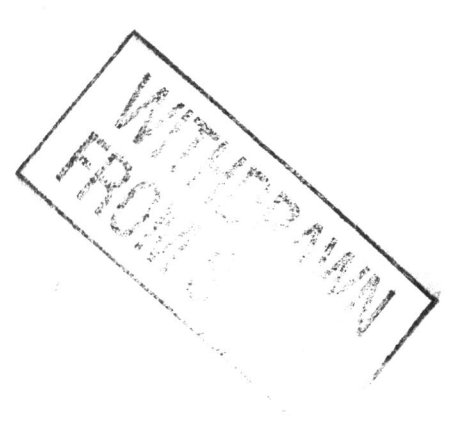

CHAPTER ONE

INTRODUCTION

At the moment there must be well over 30 published books on the subject of football hooliganism with almost every team's firm having a story to tell, as well as feature films such as The Football Factory, The Firm and Green Street, with even professional experts from top Universities giving their findings and views on the subject. This is my story; charting the escapades and running battles from the halcyon days of the early Eighties to the present day of the 2005/2006 Season; this honest and frank written account is not intended to condone or glorify football violence in any way, but to give you the reader an insight of the feelings and the emotions of running with a major firm, the importance of the terrace fashion and being part of the terrace culture. Some of the dates may not be spot on but sometimes I was too busy ducking punches to take notes so I apologise for this in advance.

I was born in May 1964, and grew up in the Rhondda valley, to a respectable working class family, my mother's family were brought up in the Rhondda valley and were proud miners, my father's family however originated from Ireland; his great grandparents were Catholic school teachers who came to the mainland during the Irish famine and settled in Deeside in North Wales. His father worked on the Settlements and struggled to bring up five small children but after the death of his wife, my father was sent to South Wales to live with his aunt.

The Rhondda valley was a very heavy industrialised area, full of miners and steelworkers, and like most welsh valleys was full of hard men and was very violent.

My childhood was a happy one I had enjoyed junior school and had plenty of friends. Having sat and passed the 11 Plus, which was the entrance qualification to the local Grammar school and the most prestigious school in the area; my future seemed to be mapped out, study hard attain O Levels and A Levels and a good career would surely follow, life was going fine, but all was to change when I entered my teenage years.

Grammar school was very imposing and was nothing like the earlier schools I had attended; you were there to work hard and misbehaviour was brutally punished some of the Masters were quite sadistic and enjoyed inflicting pain on their cowering victims; I kept my nose in the books and kept out of trouble. My first couple of years at Porth Grammar went well, I was excelling at my studies and was full of confidence. I had a number of good friends; Paul Webber was my best mate; I had known Paul most of my life he lived in the same street as my grandparents. We played most sports together but mainly football and of course tennis during Wimbledon fortnight; we were high spirited and behaved like normal eleven year olds.

As I grew older I noticed my classmates grow bigger while I remained the same and being

thirteen and very small for my age both in height and stature I acquired the nickname Mal, which was short for Malnutrition although one prick of a teacher actually thought my name was Malcolm; also around this time I acquired a bully nicknamed Tiny, simply because he wasn't, he was the biggest and hardest kid in my year, and he made the rest of my school life a nightmare. Not only did he subject me to physical violence he also ripped my school uniform and tore up all my school books. I only owned one school blazer and when I returned home with it ripped my mother hit the roof and I copped a clip around the ear. That night I couldn't sleep and went downstairs to have a piss; my old man was flat out in his favourite chair while the television blasted out. Through the corner of my eye I caught my mother, she was out our kitchen trying to sew my blazer with tears streaming down her face; not wanting her to see me I ducked into the bathroom then crept back to bed. I lay in my bed my blankets wrapped tightly to my chest as the tears slowly rolled down my cheeks and moistened my pillow; seeing my mother like that hurt me more than any of Tiny's punches ever could. When Tiny got bored of toying with me he'd get great pleasure in bullying another victim to beat me up and if I fought back he would then step in and give me a couple of digs; to him this was entertainment so I got no respite from this brutal regime. Things got so bad that I thought fuck it and I offered Tiny out for a scrap; this took a lot of courage on my part and I thought that if I fronted him maybe he'd leave me alone. The bell signalled break time and we gathered in the yard he stood there laughing egging me on I swung at him and Bang he hit me straight on the nose sending me to my knees my jumper and shirt were covered in blood; he stood over me laughing, I shuffled back to class and the bullying continued. Needless to say my school grades and education deteriorated and I spent the next three years constantly looking over my shoulder, and constantly in fear of when the next attack would come; my nerves were shot and my self-confidence had been beaten out of me; I became more insular and my friends drifted away. My teenage years and schooldays were very unhappy; at home I was brought up not to cause trouble, and was told to turn the other cheek and not make a fuss, so my bullying at school went largely unreported. Not surprisingly I left school at the earliest opportunity and with little in the way of qualifications I was destined to join the swelling ranks of the unemployed.

It was June 1980 and the recession in Britain was biting and unemployment in the valleys was forever rising.

I was sixteen, a no-hoper with no sign of steady employment, so in my spare time I enrolled at my local Gym where sessions were free to the unemployed, I wiled away the hours pumping iron, and in the evenings I joined a local boxing club, with the intention of being able to learn enough to be able to defend myself if the situation arose. Within a couple of months my whole physique changed, I was still small at 5ft 6" but I was now stocky, and my upper body was more defined and toned but still I was quiet and shy with only a small number of friends.

Punk Rock and Ska was at its height around this time and I started knocking around with lads from a rough housing estate in Trebanog a couple of them were members of the boxing club and we used to travel to Discos in local Leisure Centres and Social Clubs throughout the valley. We used to travel 20 to 30 handed and called ourselves The Banog Barmy Army; Charlie Seldon was our leader plus we had good lads like the Mortimer brothers; (Kelvin went on to become a professional boxer) plus Phillip Williams and the Stevens brothers in our ranks; they were all hard lads and had learnt to scrap at a very young age. We used to turn up at the different venues up and down the valley dressed either in Punk bondage gear with the trademark bumblebee jumpers or Crombies and Flight Jackets and bounce around to the sounds of The UK Subs, The Angellic Upstarts and The Exploited or stomped to The Specials, The Selector and Madness for the first time in years I felt safe. There would always be scuffles on the dance floors and the lights would come on and the evening would be cut short and the fighting would then continue outside; we were normally outnumbered but this didn't seem to bother us and although we sometimes got filled in we always went back for more the following week; but after a couple of months the Old Bill put a stop to the Discos and the Banog Barmy Army split up.

The harrowing events of my schooldays unknowingly caused a deep-rooted anger and rage that didn't surface until I reached eighteen and had my first taste of alcohol; I was still tormented battling thoughts of anger and hatred. Alcohol and my anger didn't mix and I became an animal, unrecognisable from the weak and timid youth I normally was, I was like a wild beast unleashed, I lashed out at anyone and everyone in my path whether they deserved it or not. I didn't care I was uncontrollable. What I didn't realise was that I had turned into something I despised, a bully. My antics were upsetting my mother and my relationship with my old man had became strained; I blamed my father for not helping me enough when I was being terrorised and I felt let down by him and although I still lived at home, I was totally detached from family life spending most of my time locked away in my bedroom only to surface at meal times. I knew that if I had carried on the way I was going I would have surely found myself in jail.

I was eighteen and I had to prove to myself that I was a man and I did this by drinking ridiculous amount of alcohol and fighting anything and everything. I was getting a bad reputation within my home town of Porth and I had been barred from a couple of local pubs, I had also made a lot of enemies and after yet another night of mindless drunken violence I ended up in the cells charged with ABH which would mean another trip to the Magistrates and the usual drill; £50 fine, £25 court costs plus £25 compensation for my victim. In the morning on my release after another

night spent soul searching I was told by the Duty Sergeant that I was the most obnoxious little man he had ever met.

There was a void in my life, I needed to belong but I didn't know where but a strange chain of events led to a change in my direction and this allowed me to channel my anger elsewhere, somewhere that violence was welcomed, I did this by joining the growing army of Football Hooligans, firstly with the Cardiff City Soul Crew and later the more violent Inter Valley Firm. I had started watching Cardiff City while at school and the passion and excitement consumed me and took away the reality of the shit I was taking at school but it was the action on the pitch the ninety minutes I loved and to be honest I was oblivious to the violence although it must have been there in the background.

The first couple of years I watched the City I travelled everywhere; I was a member of the Adar Glas Supporters Club plus I had started watching our National team abroad but Andrew Watkins my best mate at that time had started going less and less and I was noticing a new fashion on the terraces and by 1982 the Casual phenomenon had swept through Ninian Park the Soul Crew was founded and I was mixing with a new crowd. We were all kids our ages ranged from 16 to 24 the majority of my lot were 17 and 18 and we travelled the length and breadth of the British Isles in search of mayhem and madness and I finally felt I belonged I felt I was home.

CHAPTER TWO

THE NINETY MINUTES

It was 1979, and I was just fifteen when I attended my first live football match. I was still at school when Andrew Watkins asked if I would like to go with him to watch Everton in the First Round of the League Cup at Ninian Park. I hadn't really shown any interest in Cardiff City, they were an average Second Division team. My team had always been West Ham United who were a successful First Division team; mainly because they always played attractive football plus I liked their colours of claret and blue.

Though I had never been to a live match I loved football, I played for the school team and represented the Rhondda Valley and Mid Glamorgan and I would never miss Match of The Day on Saturday nights or The Big Match with Brian Moore on Sunday afternoons and then later kicking a ball around the garden re-enacting the games shown; pretending to be Stan Bowles, Tony Currie or Frank Worthington who were legends at that time.

Everton were in the First Division, so they would have plenty of household names in their side plus I thought it would be a good distraction from the shit I was going through at school.

It was an evening kick off so we caught the train from Porth, the train was packed, everyone decked out in blue and white, I had no idea Cardiff City had such a large following from the valleys. The 15 Mile journey seemed to take forever, we finally arrived at Cardiff Central Station, we made our way outside the vast station, this was my first visit to Cardiff without my parents; I suppose I was a bit sheltered, I asked Andrew if he knew the way to Ninian Park he said "Just follow the crowd", and laughed.

We made our way down Tudor Road and towards the ground, we were part of a huge crowd slowly snaking its way through the busy Cardiff streets, it was early September so it was still quite light, it was quite a warm evening and as we neared the ground there in the distance were the large floodlights, I felt the first signs of excitement, a kind of fluttering in my stomach.

We bought a programme each and I bought a scarf, which copying everyone else I tied around my wrist, we followed the crowd onto the bob bank and took our places on the packed terrace and with thirty minutes to kick off we soaked up the pre-match atmosphere. The Bob Bank was all terracing; that was where the City faithful congregated and as they cranked up the noise with chants of "Bloooobirds! Bloooobirds!" it was deafening we could hardly hear each other speak.

It was a very open match with both teams going close, but neither team could break the deadlock, chances fell at either end and there was very little to choose between the two teams. Time was running out and the game was tied at 0 - 0, I was enthralled, I was lost in the incredible atmosphere, which made an everlasting impression on myself, suddenly Andrew nudged me,

"C'mon", he said and led me to the exit, "But the game isn't finished", I protested he explained that we needed to avoid the crowds if we were going to catch our train home.

We started to force our way through the swaying crowds towards the exit, when out of nowhere there was pandemonium, with people hugging and kissing each other, the Bob Bank bounced as one, fans young and old caught up in these amazing scenes. When the chaos died down I learned Cardiff had been awarded a penalty, and with only a few minutes remaining a goal now would surely kill off this first leg. Billy Ronson stepped up to take the penalty, he faced George Wood in goal, and there was a strange silence around the ground my heart was in my mouth. Ronson took a small run up and placed the ball to Wood's left, and to our disbelief and horror George Wood got his hands on the ball and parried it away to safety. There was silence all around apart from the Everton fans in the bottom enclosure that were delirious.

The referee blew the final whistle a few minutes later and Andrew and myself left the ground, we had to put a sprint on, to get back to Cardiff Central in time for our train. For the next couple of days Cardiff City dominated my life, I couldn't get that night out of my head, I was hooked, and even though I was going through hell at school nothing had the same importance as the ninety minutes.

That season of 1979-80 Andrew and myself attended well over half of Cardiff City's home games, but one match stood out from all the rest. That was the visit of Chelsea.

As far as Andrew and myself were concerned this was to be another normal Saturday fixture. We left home the same time, boarded the 1:10 train, which consisted of six carriages packed equally with weekend shoppers and City fans, many of which were Skinheads wearing the usual attire of Harrington jackets, bleached jeans and Fourteen Hole oxblood coloured Doc Martins, others were decked out in white Butcher coats these were very imposing blokes, and to be honest I didn't really feel comfortable in their presence.

We arrived as usual at Cardiff Central Station, and made our way to the ground, everything seemed normal, with nothing out of the ordinary. We entered the Bob Bank, up the slight slope, and we made our way to our usual spot under the T.V. gantry, that was where all the singing started, but this area was a lot fuller than usual, so we decided to sit on the back wall.

We had just settled down in our new vantage point and were checking our programmes when, "Video Killed the Radio Star", by The Buggles started blasting out of the P.A. System, then suddenly everyone's eyes were drawn to the corner of the Bob Bank, towards the catering van that was perched between the Visitor's Grange End and the Bob Bank.

Two dozen or so battle hardened Cockneys had made their way onto the Bob Bank via the Grange End entrance with the intention of taking our end, once on the Bob Bank they started giving it the big un and soon found themselves facing a wall of City fans, a flurry of boots and punches knocked the Chelsea backwards and they were forced towards the back wall, they were now cornered with nowhere to run. From what I could see they were overwhelmed by the sheer numbers, the City fans swarmed all over them like flies over shit and I could see amongst the baying Cardiff mob blokes who had been on our train earlier in the day. The boots and punches continued to rain down and the police seemed very slow to react and some of the Chelsea had now resorted to throwing themselves headlong over the wall onto the concrete below, while others were unceremoniously thrown over by City fans, others just rolled up and took a kicking until the police arrived, once order was restored what was left of the Chelsea lads were escorted back to the Visitors Enclosure with chants of, "Cardiff Aggro", and "You'll never take the Bob Bank", ringing in their ears.

The game itself was boring by comparison and I can only just remember the score, we lost 2-0. That was my first sight of football hooliganism. This was an age of innocence for Andrew and myself, we liked to be inside the ground a good half hour before kick off and we used to rush straight back to the station and straight home on the final whistle of each game, so we were oblivious to what went on in Cardiff after matches and I quickly dismissed this behaviour as a one off.

That 1979-1980 Season drew to a close and that was the only disorder I saw. The next season was to herald a new era, Andrew and I started to attend away matches and we finished the season just missing a handful of games both home and away, we were now truly loyal supporters.

CHAPTER THREE

FOLLOWERS OF FASHION

As I've already stated, I started watching Cardiff City in 1979 with Andrew Watkins, we were both 15 years old and we saw the last few home games of the season, and we were hooked. That summer dragged by, the start of the new season was always on our minds, it couldn't come fast enough.

The 1981 season heralded new experiences, we attended our first away game, Torquay United in the First Round of the League Cup; the atmosphere and camaraderie were fantastic and sent shivers down our spines. After that experience we both vowed to attend as many away games as possible and amazingly we managed to miss only six games all season. The majority of fans travelled by road, either on Supporter's coaches or hired transit vans or minibuses, we travelled with Adar Glas (Bluebirds) Supporter's Club that was run by Roy and Mair Daniels.

The fashion on the terraces at this time was; the Skinhead or Suede-head hair-cut, tight T-shirts, lightweight Harrington style jackets, skin-tight bleached jeans, Dr Martin boots and your team's scarf tied around your right wrist, in winter heavy donkey jackets replaced the more lightweight jackets. I guess we must have looked a scruffy bunch of so and sos and quite intimidating when in large numbers.

All this was about to change, and the first I noticed of this new trend was in 1981 when I was walking through Hannah Street, in Porth. There were a couple of older lads who followed English football teams, these were: - Julian Trajic who followed Everton; his brother Donald who followed Aston Villa and John Harris who followed Man United; they were sporting heavy wedge haircuts that fell behind the ears but over one eye, smart adidas polo shirts, skin tight stonewashed Fiorucci jeans, which were worn long enough to put a two inch split in the bottom so that they lay neatly over your trainers; this fashion had originated in the North West of England, and Liverpool in particular. The Scousers had enjoyed major success in Europe and the Scallies had robbed their way across the major cities of Europe lifting the latest designer sportswear and this new look was now sweeping its way through the football fraternity. These lads certainly stood out from the crowd, and this was the first time I realised that there was so much more to football than just the ninety minutes, and I desperately wanted to be part of it.

In those early days I personally found it very difficult to find out where to buy the latest labels, I had very little confidence and I found it really difficult to talk to those older lads. The price of those clothes for a 17 year old earning just £23.50 a week on a Youth Training Scheme, were way out of my league. In the early Eighties Cardiff only had a few stores that sold the "gear",

Robert Barker sold Lacoste, Austin Reed sold Pringle and Lyle & Scott, while Woodies in the early days stocked more labels than you could shake a stick at and Olympus Sport on Queen Street sold Tacchini, Fila, Ellesse plus all the major trainers. If you wanted any other label you had to travel further a field.

My mates and I, like most lads of that time had Student Railcards which gave us 25% Discount, we used to save up and go to such fashion emporiums as Woodhouse, Reiss and Jones in London, but this wasn't without its problems and you always had the fear of being taxed as you came across lads from the major Cockney firms. We always travelled in twos or threes not to draw too much attention to ourselves, and the thought of coming unstuck just added to the excitement, the whole shopping experience was one long Buzz.

Slowly the face of the terraces started to change and a legion of footy fans up and down the country were sporting this new look and even in my home village of Porth deep in the Rhondda valley there were like-minded lads coming out of the woodwork.

By 1982 the Soul Crew was formed, I was 18 and until now I had been relatively unaware of football violence, and I certainly didn't see myself as being a part of it. With the excitement brought by the emergence of the Soul Crew, I stopped travelling with Andrew, he was wary of the violence; he sensed a change was coming. He later moved from the Rhondda Valley, his family resettled in Porthcawl, a popular seaside town.

The Soul Crew was made up of mainly 16 to 24 year olds, the majority being from Cardiff, with smaller groups coming from the surrounding valleys, plus lads from Bridgend, Port Talbot and Neath. All sporting neat wedge haircuts, Lacoste polo shirts, Pringle golfing jumpers, stone-washed Lois jeans with split hems, white trainers and Patrick Macs; we were like clones, and a more sinister side of football was about to raise its ugly head. We no longer travelled by road but opted to travel by Intercity trains, taking advantage of Student and Family Railcards, as well as Persil Vouchers; we travelled all over the country at least 200 strong.

There had been documented football violence throughout the seventies but this was different, organised firms were being formed and springing up throughout Britain such as the West Ham ICF, Chelsea Head-hunters, Birmingham Zulu Warriors, Millwall Bushwhackers, Portsmouth 6.57 Crew and Man Utd's Red Army who were the biggest hooligan firm in the country, and every Saturday afternoon these rival gangs would bump into each other on train stations up and down the country. These firms were more sophisticated and the violence was more organised, and more ferocious, with more and more firm members carrying blades. The favoured weapon was the Stanley knife introduced by the Scousers.

The clothes you wore to the game played just an important part as the violence, with lads purchasing a new set of clothes for the bigger games and the biggest put down was if a rival firm called you Gypos or if you turned up and you looked out dated. This could happen quite easily as a new designer came to the fore; in 1982 & 1983 fashions came in and out so quickly that no one label or look would last long, in the space of a football season you would go through about three different looks; us younger lads would look up to the top boys and copy the labels they were wearing, but normally by the time you had perfected the look they would have moved on.

I remember Carlisle's Border Firm coming to Ninian Park in 1983, we were still wearing Lyle & Scott and Pringle jumpers while they were sporting tracksuit tops, introducing makes like; Fila, Ellesse and Sergio Tacchini, they were about fifteen strong and had set out on the 4.30 a.m. train I really respect firms like that, they had a crap team at that time but still travelled all that way and what I saw of them they were no mugs and showed no fear.

The end of the 1983 season we started moving away from the sporty tennis and golf wear and onto more up market designers such as Giorgio Armani, his range of knitwear was very popular at this time, matched with Aquascutum or Burberry house check shirts, Farah trousers, leather Italian shoes and Burberry golfing jackets, topped off with a Deer Stalker hat, I even remember some lads carrying walking canes to matches.

We thought we were the business and more importantly than that the police never gave us a second glance as we took our seats in the Grandstand week after week. The Grandstand was the only section of Ninian Park non-segregated and was very sparsely policed.

Portsmouth came to Cardiff in 1983 and bowled into the Grandstand at around 2:30 p.m. they were about 60 strong; they looked much older than us, I noticed some were wearing Burberry trench coats, taunting us with their Nova Check, complimented with smart Farah trousers and Hush Puppies suede desert boots. We were still a relatively young firm and we had gathered at the top of the A Stand looking down on the Pompey, we had the advantage of being higher up the stand and as both sets of fans met in the middle there was a lot of gesticulating and bouncing around until the first punches were thrown, then we set about each other going toe to toe, one on ones breaking out all over the stand, with the older lads from both mobs taking the lead, a lad called Pringle was one of the first of our lot into the fray followed by a couple of Barry boys, the rest of us piled down the stand jumping over the wooden seats and straight into our adversaries; I came face to face with a lad sporting a blonde wedge and a Salmon coloured Pringle jumper; he looked unmistakeably English and was jumping around in front of me; I moved forward and Bang! Hit him right on the button; he winced and his face reddened and quick as you like I hit him again and this time he beat a hasty retreat; there was a kind of a muffled roar and you could here the punches and boots connecting. There's no better feeling than connecting properly and knowing your man is hurt, and because of the lack of a police presence it kicked off for about two minutes and anyone who's been involved in football violence knows how much damage can be done in that time, both firms stood their ground not giving an inch and the adrenalin was pumping, the police arrived and separated the warring factions and peace was restored, the 6:57 Crew were escorted out of the Grandstand and into their away section, we had done ourselves proud and personally I thought the honours ended just about even. This was the first real violence I had been involved in and I was shocked by the realisation that although there were around 100 lads congregated together only a dozen of each side actually got involved and although I was frightened, the thrill was indescribable, I felt so many emotions at once and remarkably after a tentative and hesitant baptism I was pretty shocked that I held my own against older and bigger lads, and I learned an invaluable lesson that you don't need to be a hard man you just have to be able to display plenty of bottle.

Over the coming decades the football fashion went hand in hand with the hooligan element and although styles and fashions changed, the faces in the crew remained constant. However, not all the fashions were smart, and there was definitely a North/South divide in styles. The southern styles were much smarter, I recall Aquascutum blazers, Pierre Cardin shirts, Armani and Gucci silk ties, Chinos and Bally shoes being very popular with London lads; I also remember some ridiculous looks; paisley shirts, dungarees, ponchos and deck shoes stick in my mind.

From the mid eighties to the early nineties; when the rave and Manchester scenes were in full swing the footy fashion took a radical change of direction, once again its origin was from the North West of England; In 1985 "The Scruff Look", took hold, this comprised of hooded corduroy jackets, heavy knit fisherman jumpers, semi-flared jeans and heavy duty walking shoes such as Timberland or Rockport; also tweed hunting jackets were very popular and labels such as Barbour, Peter Storm and Berghaus came to the fore. I personally loved this look because there were only a handful of us in the valley dressed like this; we looked like street urchins and got plenty of strange looks from the locals. I remember standing in Porth's main shopping centre wearing a tweed jacket, a Marks & Spencer lambs wool crew neck jumper, 16 inch flared cords, a pair of specs I'd acquired from some charity shop while puffing on a pipe. I remember quite vividly my father threatening to have me committed under The Mental Health Act. Sometimes it was a case of the more outrageous the outfit the better, other trends at this time were: - back perm haircuts, Gee 2 jumpers with the badge on the arm similar to Armani, Benetton Rugby shirts, leather and suede patchwork jumpers with draw string necks, these were purchased from Cardiff's Indoor Market also around this time many lads started wearing Burberry and Aquascutum Scarves wrapped around their faces masking their appearance.

In 1986 I started to follow Man United quite regularly, and the major labels seen on the K Stand at the start of the 1986 season were: - Ocean Pacific Tee shirts and sweatshirts, Marc O'Polo, John Smedley, Ball and C17 jeans plus Timberland shoes. During the winter months came the appearance of Luhta cagoules that were immortalised by English fans deported from Luxembourg and would always be known as the Luxembourg rowing coat by my mates and I. Cockneys on the other hand were sporting Paisley shirts and Dungarees, sweaters from Next, other favourite labels were Chevignon, Chipie and Radio plus gelled back hairstyles were very popular.

Early Nineties, the majority of us were now in our mid twenties and this was a pivotal time, many of our main players were getting married and having kids or forging ahead with their careers; they took advantage of the exploding Dance Scene, some got into D-Jing or promoting Raves and Gigs, others got into the drugs market while others got into the security business, while the straighter heads of the firm committed most of their time to their day jobs. Around this time a lot of our top lads turned their back on the football violence; this wasn't only confined to Cardiff but was happening all across Britain. I personally never left the scene but I did stop following Cardiff and followed United instead, I loved the Manchester scene; The Stone Roses and Happy Mondays and although the clubs were awash with E's getting loved up on the Weekends never appealed to me; I never needed that kind of buzz. Although there was undoubtedly a lull in the activities of the major firms at this time, the violence never totally disappeared it just took place on a smaller scale.

It was around this time the terrace culture embraced the Italian designer Massimo Osti's creations; jackets with full face balaclavas and built in goggles, labels such as Massimo Osti Production, World Wide Web, Left Hand, Boneville, CP Company and Stone Island. The price of these labels and their styles made the "football look" unique, with lads only too happy to pay £750 for jackets and £250 plus for knitwear.

Personally, I was happiest wearing dark hooded jackets, an Aquascutum scarf to obscure my face, dark coloured heavy knitwear, dark boot-cut Paul Smith jeans and Timberland boots, late Autumn or Winter were my favourite times of the year, the pitch of night at evening matches, dancing in and out of the shadows picking off the away lads; the police were normally unable to distinguish between the two sets of supporters, and many an away supporter came unstuck.

Nowadays on the terraces, Mulberry, Iceberg, Mandarina Duck, Prada and Paul & Shark are very popular, but you can't beat classic lines like Aquascutum and Burberry; also Stone Island and CP Company are still the must have hooligan accessories, although after the death of Massimo Osti in 2005 the recent quality of Stone Island and CP Company productions have left a lot to be desired and copies and fakes have flooded the market place and the younger wannabes at Ninian

Park can be seen in their Clone Island gear. We are all either in our late thirties or early forties now with thinning hair and beer bellies, as well as all being family men, but we can still be seen returning to the place of our youth every other Saturday afternoon, still with an eye for the fashion, and the chance of a bit of nonsense.

Desperate Days

This was Thatcherite Britain and growing up in the Rhondda valley in the early eighties was hard and depressing there were very little employment opportunities, so I had to live on my wits, I always kept an eye out for ways to supplement my Giro, this was common practice for most of us. We all liked the footy, all being active members of the Soul Crew and we all liked to be seen wearing the latest footy gear, especially in times of depression good clothes gave the perception of affluence so we had to get cash from somewhere because in reality none of us had a pot to piss in.

There were four of us: - Cen, who was 19 and was a jobbing plasterer who was out of work more than in; Johnny who was 20 and attending Dental College; Dukey, who was 22 and the oldest, his last job was school milk monitor; and myself, I was also 20 and flitting aimlessly from one job to another. Here are a few of the escapades we got involved in during the depression years of the early eighties.

Legitimate money was always hard to come by but there was always money to be made if you were prepared to take risks. One such occasion was a blazing July lunchtime, Cen and I were walking through High Street in Porth, when we spotted an orange cement mixer unattended on the pavement of number 34, Cen nudged me, "we'll be having that", I looked at him blankly, "C'mon, Dickey in the club is after one", our pace quickened, we reached number 34 the front door was open, we peered in, not a sound, so we both lifted the mixer and silently but speedily had it away. Once we had safely left High Street we lowered it onto its wheels and proceeded to wheel it through the streets, what a noise it made and the looks we got off passers-by were a picture, how we kept straight faces I don't know.

We wheeled the mixer to the Working Men's' Club, Cen entered and sought Dickey, Cen returned, "C'mon he's playing snooker", so we lifted the mixer up the few front steps, through the large double doors, passed the Committee men and into the snooker hall, Dickey was dumbstruck, so shocked he missed his pot, he gratefully handed over £80 which we split and enjoyed the rest of the day on the pop.

We weren't bad lads, but we weren't averse to bending the law either, there were other occasions when easy money presented itself to us. There was a new housing estate being built in Hopkinstown a few miles from us, this was the first of its kind in our area and Cen roped Johnny and I into his latest scam. Cen had worked on many building sites and his experience was to be invaluable. Johnny was the only driver among us, the rest of us were either too bladdered or stoned to drive, so he hired a van for the day and picked us up at 8.00 a.m. sharp.

We drew up to the site, there were a few workmen dotted around, Cen asked, "Where's the plumbing gear kept", "See Jim, he's down in that hut", he pointed to a large wooden green shed, Johnny drove us down through the muddy site, Cen and I jumped out of the van and entered the shed, "You must be Jim", said Cen, Jim nodded, "We need three boilers, pipes and fittings", Cen continued, he had more front than Blackpool that lad, Jim pointed to a back storage room, "Help yourselves", I sheepishly followed Cen my heart raced, the thought of being caught filled my head. The back room was like an Aladdin's cave filled with thousands of pounds worth of equipment. We both took hold of a large copper boiler and made our way to our waiting van, Johnny smiled, "I'll give you a hand", and ran to open the back doors, one by one we loaded the three copper boilers and the piping and fittings required into the back of the van. Cen signed for the materials and we bade farewell to Jim and slowly set off up the building site desperately trying not to look suspicious, we passed gangs of workmen oblivious to our cunning stunt and calmly drove through the large gates of the site and away back to our home village where Smithy the Scrappy paid us £150 per boiler, copper was like gold in those days. That particular scam paid for a selection of Marks & Spencer lambs wool crew necks a couple of pairs of Farah slacks as well as a loose perm form Neil George's Hair Salon in Porth.

Out of all us lads, the only real thief was Dukey, or the Duke as he preferred to be called. He would tell anyone who would listen, he got his nickname after the Duke of Earl who was immortalised by the band Darts, but the truth was; in the Rhondda like other deprived areas, skint parents would buy their children sandals in the winter and Wellington boots in the summer. This singled out the wearer for ridicule and Dukey was one such child and got the name the Duke of Wellington.

Duke was a very unsuccessful thief and was as bright as a power cut, but when it came to Cardiff City he was fanatical, he thought nothing of hitch-hiking to away games or arriving at away towns a couple of days before a match, sleeping on train stations until the day of the game; personally I had a lot of respect for him, I saw him as more of a loveable rogue and he used to be a frequent visitor to my house, my dad would joke, "Nail down the valuables there's a thief about", to which Dukey would reply, "don't bother, there's nothing worth nicking Mr Gough". My dad was very much aware of Dukey's light fingers but had no idea of my little scams, until, one Autumnal evening there was a knock on our door, there stood Dukey, hands full of assorted leather and suede jackets, I was horrified, "What are you doing with them?" I asked, "I need somewhere safe to store them", "No way", I continued "My old man won't have that", my dad was a strict Catholic and always lived within the law, "Go on ask him", he insisted, I entered the living room with my hands full of jackets, my father was sat in his favourite chair, he gave me a long hard stare, "Dad", I started sheepishly, "Can Dukey keep these here for a couple of days please?" "Nicked are they?" he asked, "You know Dukey", I replied, "He hasn't got anywhere else", I continued, my father then went through his speech of how people who handle stolen goods get into more trouble than the actual thief, I gave him a knowing smile, "Where is he then?" dad asked, "Waiting at the door", "Ask him in", he ordered, I called to the door, "Come in Duke, my father wants a word", Dukey entered sheepishly his toothless grin filled his face, "Alright Mr Gough", he mumbled, "What's with these jackets then Duke?", "Nothing, I just need somewhere to put them, only for a couple of days", Duke said innocently, my father took a good look at the jackets and to my surprise said, "O.K. Duke, just a couple of days, but I want one of the leathers for my trouble", crafty sod I thought, Dukey quickly agreed, and they lived in the bottom of my wardrobe. Duke was good to his word, but the jackets were of really crap quality and Duke got lumbered with them.

Another of Duke's misadventures came when a new store opened in the village; Flairs was the name. The store's main revenue came from a photography service but they also sold top of the range cameras, microscopes and telescopes. Duke broke in and managed to get away with a vast haul, and over the following weeks he managed to dispose of the items. One top of the range telescope was left and this was the topic of conversation when we all met up at the Llwyncelyn Hotel for our usual Friday night out. Overhearing our conversation, Jack Williams, an elderly regular chipped in, "Why don't you sell it back to the shop, they must need a replacement?" we all stared in disbelief, not sure if he was serious or pulling our legs. The beer flowed and the night progressed and no more was thought of old Jack's inane suggestion.

Unknown to the rest of us, the following morning Dukey made his way to Flairs in Hannah Street, with telescope in tow, he waited for the store to empty and attempted to sell the telescope. The owner examined the telescope closely, he must have thought he was dreaming, he made Dukey an offer but told Dukey to take a seat while he went to the safe to get the money, once in his office he phoned the police, meanwhile Dukey waited patiently in the waiting room. The police arrived and Dukey was arrested, and Dukey was left wondering how he had been caught, serial numbers never entered his head.

Our most profitable scam started off as a legitimate job, Cen had arranged a day's work for us, we were to gut and re-plaster a Butcher's shop in Taffs Well. Again we hired a van, Johnny was the driver, we arrived at the store around 8.00 a.m. it was having a full refit, we were to rip out the existing counter and fittings, re-plaster the walls and make good before the shop fitters and carpenters arrived. It was a bigger job than I thought, it consisted of a lot of heavy lifting, we stacked up the old equipment and Cen started the plastering, I was his labourer for the day,

Johnny didn't like to get his hands too dirty.

The Plastering was finished, Davies the Butcher was very happy with our work, he gave Cen our pay, he looked at the fittings and old equipment stacked on the pavement and asked Cen to weigh the materials in at a scrap merchants, Cen agreed, we headed back to the van, Davies had obviously dealt with Cen before, he reappeared with a meat cleaver in his hand, "Get a good price, and we split it three ways, you cross me and I'll cut your ears off", he was deadly serious. We clambered into the van; Cen looked at me, placed his hands over his ears and asked, "How do I look?" "O.K.", I replied, "Then fuck him", we laughed uncontrollably, and Johnny took us to Smithy the Scrappy who gave us £450 for the lot, "Not bad for a days work", smiled Cen. Those days were hard but incredibly fun, we lived life for the moment and snatched every opportunity with both hands; without those scams we wouldn't have gone to half the matches we did and we certainly wouldn't have afforded the latest fashions. Time has taken its toll, we are all in our late thirties or early forties now and no longer see each other, we have all moved on with our separate lives, our lives are a lot duller now but a lot more stable. I often look back with fondness at the scrapes we got in, and wonder where the others are today.

CHAPTER FOUR

THE WHEELS ON YOUR HOUSE GO ROUND AND ROUND

The title of this chapter refers to our local rivals Swansea City, the Gypos of South Wales or the Jack bastards, as they are affectionately known. Over the years I've been involved in many a toe to toe with our local adversaries. More than any other team, here are a few of the running battles we have enjoyed over the past decades.

The Battle of The Badminton

The first local derby I travelled to was in the mid 80's, the Soul Crew was by now well established, in the early days the police were much more relaxed, there were no restriction of travel and we were able to make our own way to the match. The mass exodus to the west was on. At this time there was a valleys Cardiff fan named Lloyd Griffiths who was managing The Badminton public house, a small back street boozer just a short walk from the Vetch and he had invited a small band of Rhondda valley and Pontypridd lads to join him for a drink before the game. This was the worst kept secret ever, with every valley lad intending to make his way to The Badminton.

We descended on the Swansea Town Centre train station; hundreds of us kitted out in colourful designer polo shirts and stonewashed Lois jeans. The Cardiff lads sought the city centre bars while us valley lads made our way through the Swansea back streets to The Badminton. Pughy, Slocombe, Macey and myself arrived around 12:30; the pub was already rammed with familiar faces drinking both inside and out. We got ourselves a couple of pints and joined the army of lads outside basking in the glorious sunshine.

At about 2 O'clock the pub started to empty with many lads making their way to the Vetch, around forty of us stayed put with the majority still supping outside, after a short while a group of about fifteen blokes made their way through the throng of drinkers and into the bar, these were older blokes, not dressers more akin to beer-monsters, we figured they were older valleys blokes and thought no more of it.

They got their beers in and made their way to the Pool Room at the end of the bar; playing pool were Leighton and his mate plus a couple of our lads watching. Suddenly all hell broke loose this group were obviously Jacks and having the numbers had attacked the four lads. From outside we heard the smashing of glasses, so we charged inside where we were met with a hail of pint glasses and pool balls, in all the pandemonium I could see two of ours lying on the floor one was

Leighton, he had been smashed around the head with a cue which had split his ear in two. The noise was deafening, I could hear the barmaid's screams over the smashing glasses that still rained down on us. The Jacks were bouncing and screaming at us and calling us on, but the glasses weren't coming at us so often now, and picking up tables and chairs we steamed into them forcing them back against the far wall of the pub, now we had the upper hand, one fat Jack in his Matalan's finest was decked by a stool in his mush, and as he went down he received a fucking good shoeing, Sicey managed to wrestle the pool cue out of a Jack's hand and proceeded to beat him over the head with it, and even though we were in the heat of battle, witnessing that made me laugh so much, I almost dropped the chair I was holding. Our superior numbers were starting to tell with tables and chairs being put over Jack heads, it was like a scene out of a Western movie, Melvyn from Barry was right in the thick of it raining a flurry of punches into a group that were huddled together, I used my chair to good effect, using it to send Jacks scurrying out of my reach, the tables had by now completely turned, the Jacks were frantically trying to defend themselves and deflect our blows from causing serious damage, we were now taking the fight to them, in the close proximity of the small Pool Room the fighting was up close and personal. The battle of The Badminton lasted about ten minutes before the Old Bill arrived parting the warring factions and picking up the battered, one of them being Leighton; they escorted the Jacks out of the pub and as they did so Macey was giving plenty of verbal and when one Jack responded to his taunts Macey lunged through the police escort and duly got nicked for threatening behaviour and that was the end of his day out.

Once the Jacks had been led away and the dust had settled we went back inside. The amount of damage caused was unbelievable poor Lloyd was left shaking his head at the bar, we helped him tidy up the best we could before setting off for the match. The rest of the day passed off without incident, but this wasn't going to be the last time I'd mix it with the Jacks.

The Queens Crew

We were playing Swansea quite regularly in the mid to late Eighties, and you could guarantee that at the Vetch you would have a row and this time would be no different. Once again we made our way to Swansea by service train, around 400 of us making the short trip west. At the station we were met by a large police presence, we were ushered out of the station and towards the ground, using the back streets to avoid the city centre.

The Swansea Old Bill weren't as proactive as Cardiff's and our escort was allowed to string out, and as we neared the Vetch we took our chance, around thirty of us slipped the escort, including Ashley, Cen and myself. We made our way to The Queens public house just a stone throws away from the Vetch, that was where the Jack firm drank. The Jacks didn't have the numbers of Cardiff but were a tight knit firm and their hatred of Cardiff is well documented.

We turned the corner into the large street; we could see The Queens on the corner. We picked up the pace trying to reach the front doors before being spotted, unfortunately, as we neared the doors the Jacks came steaming out tooled up with pint glasses and bottles, we backed off into the middle of the road with glasses and bottles raining down on us, the Jacks spread out along the road, we knew this was our only chance of a bit of nonsense, so we had to act a bit sharpish before the Old Bill arrived.

Both firms confronted each other, and attacked each other head on. The Jacks looked a lot older than us with moustaches and thinning hair, but that didn't put us off as we charged into each other, both groups giving as good as they got, after a quick skirmish we had them on the back foot and some of their lads had clearly had enough and darted back to the safety of The Queens, the lads that were left in the street were rounded on and a couple were sent reeling to the floor by a couple of right-handers and at that moment the Old Bill arrived like a bad smell, rounded us up and proceeded to escort us from the area, at this point The Queens' doors flew open and the Jacks let fly once more with pint glasses and bottles crashing around our heads and chants of "Jack Army!, Jack Army!", ringing in our ears. This was a desperate act of bravado for they knew that they had come off second best.

As the Old Bill led us away to the Visiting section of the Vetch we were all relieved that the Old Bill didn't make any arrests, they were happy to chuck us in the ground and out of their hair.

The Welsh Cup

The next time we played Swansea City was when we were drawn together in the Welsh Cup, to
be played on a Tuesday night. Around this time I had been travelling to the footy with a tight
group of lads who were known as The I.V.F. (The Inter Valley Firm) a splinter group of the Soul
Crew. The main faces were Keith, Rees, Adie and his brother Mark, the Foster brothers as well
as Turkey, Oz and Bitten whom I had brought into the fold. The police had started clamping
down on us travelling by this time so we arranged to travel from Pontyclun to Neath by train then
transferring to a fleet of taxis to ferry us into Swansea itself.

I arrived at the Bute public house early afternoon, inside were Simon, Ambler, Keith, Rees, Adie,
Foster of Taffs Well, Hicksy, Summers, Bexy Trueman, Digger, Wurzel and a couple of others,
our numbers totalled twenty five, about average numbers for The I.V.F. On good days we could
call on fifty lads stretching from Llantrisant, Taffs Well, Pontypridd plus the Rhondda, Cynon
and Rhymney Valleys.

We boarded the train, there were about hundred lads already aboard, we made sure we didn't
mingle with them and sat in a quiet compartment at the rear of the train, accompanying us were a
dozen transport police, as we pulled into Bridgend station another thirty lads piled on, next stop
was Neath. We pulled into Neath station; we could see around twenty lads waiting to board, we
made our exit from the train as the Neath lads boarded and made our way to the station exits. Sat
outside were two Old Bill in a patrol car, not making eye contact we made our way to the town
centre and split into different boozers from where we phoned local taxis.

The local plod left us alone and we set off to Swansea in a fleet of seven taxis. We were dropped
off in a side street just off the Central Stand, that is where we were heading, the Jacks had begun
sitting in there and we were going to surprise them. We noticed that a mob of about twenty Jacks
were queuing at the turnstiles with two Old Bill in close attendance, so we decided to amble up to
the entrance gates in groups of twos and threes not to draw attention to ourselves, but the old
codger on the gate was taking an age, and we soon began to mingle with the Jacks, the look on
their faces showed we had been sussed. The Old Bill picked up on this vibe and started to
twitch, they asked Digger where we were from and cool as ice he told them Llansamlet, (a small
West Walian village). That satisfied the curiosity of the Old Bill and the old codger finally got
his finger out and we started to make our way into the ground.

On the inside the stares and strange looks continued, we grouped up just inside the entrance while
most of the Jacks climbed the steps into the stand. Our numbers grew as more of us entered the
ground; Wurzel was the last in, he came in sandwiched between two Jacks and one of them gave

him a sly couple of digs as we looked on, that was one - nil to them, we could have easily stepped in and filled those wankers in, but that would have drawn attention to ourselves. We wanted to wait until we were on the stand before kicking off.

The plan was to march onto the stand together as one; but I needed a piss, so the lads hung around, Keith must have had the same idea. We both entered the run down piss house and stood either side of one of the Jacks from outside, as soon as he saw us his face dropped and before he could fuck off we gave him a sharp clip around the ear and a swift boot up the arse. We joined the other lads with thoughts of climbing the rackety iron steps into the Jack end.

The Jacks appeared at the top of the steps, our eyes locked; Wurzel, Rees and Adie were the first up the steps and the braver Jacks came hurtling down into us. After a couple of punches from our lads their advances stopped and we pushed them back up the steps and back into the stand, we advanced up the steps taking them two at a time but at the top were a group of stewards backed up by the Old Bill who pushed us back down and out of the ground.

Once again the Swansea police surprised us by transferring us to the visitors section, personally I thought a one way ticket to the cells was on the cards, as we passed the curious copper from earlier, Digger gave him a wry smile.

The Littlewoods Cup 1988

The next time we met was a Littlewoods Cup tie, in 1988, also an evening kick off, I had arranged to meet Rob and Paul Foster in the Admiral in Taffs Well, when I arrived Paul and his uncle Granville were already bladdered, this was going to be an interesting trip I thought. We made our way in Paul's works van, not a very comfortable journey sitting on bags of plaster and the like while trying to keep my clothes clean.

We had arranged to meet Keith, Rees and the others outside the Central Stand, it was a dark autumnal evening when we reached Swansea, I had my hooded leather jacket firmly done up and my Aquascutum scarf wrapped tightly around my face sheltering from the cold. We met the others and made our way into the ground, to our surprise there were no Jack lads to be seen just straight-heads; after having a quick look around we climbed the steps into the old fashioned stand and took our seats towards the front. Our numbers weren't great there were twenty of us plus another ten lads from Bridgend.

The game kicked off, it was a pretty low-key affair on the pitch, while the atmosphere off it was electric. There were about eight hundred Cardiff housed in the visiting section behind the goal, and the Jacks had congregated on the North Bank to the side of them, obscenities and threats were spewed to and fro, while the thirty of us looked on.

Well into the second half Cardiff scored to break the deadlock this led to a mini pitch invasion from us and after congratulating the scorer I ran over to Frankie Burrows the manager of the time to shake his hand but all I got was a clip around the head for my troubles, we left the pitch and once again returned to our seats in the stand. On spotting us in the Central Stand the Jacks mobbed up and once the North Bank gates were opened a group of two dozen lads left the stadium and navigated their way through the deserted Swansea streets and avoiding the attentions of the Old Bill they made their way to the Central Stand. The first we knew of this was when two dozen lads rushed us from behind, all their main lads were there and the Bridgend lads felt the brunt of the attack as the Jacks steamed into them. We flew up the aisle into our rivals while the rest of our lot piled over the wooden seats and in the panic the Jacks managed to give some of our lads a slap, both mobs went at it hammer and tongs. The Old Bill rushed up the stand to restore order; we regrouped and were able to push the Jacks out of the stand, Ginger from Bridgend leading the charge, this little skirmish was over before it had really began and we left the ground pretty frustrated.

We returned to our van which was parked by the Leisure Centre and we could see scuffles breaking out all over the car park, this was the Jacks speciality picking off stragglers, we stood outside the van watching and waiting and then a group of three lads came running towards us between the parked cars, as they passed us we gave them a couple of slaps and sent them on their way.

Once the mayhem had died down we set off for home but the Jacks had other ideas and as we travelled under one of the many bridges that span the road an almighty rock crashed against the windscreen sending shards of glass into the driver and passenger seats, the van careered out of control for a moment before Rob managed to regain control. From the side of the road we could see the silhouettes of the Jack bastards fleeing into the night.

We returned to Swansea and reported the incident to the local plod, Paul and Rob were livid and we wanted revenge, we emptied the tools from Paul's van, we had carpet knives, sledge hammers and trowels we must have looked a right sight as we made our way through the deserted city streets looking for Jacks to batter. Luckily no one crossed our path and the plod were happy for us to drive the van home. We drove home with the wind whistling through the smashed windscreen and that was the coldest journey I've ever made.

Firm on the Run

Our next meeting was a league match, a Bank Holiday afternoon. Travelling to Swansea by train was out of the question that would have brought a large police escort and led us straight into the ground, so we had arranged to travel by car. There was a convoy of twenty cars by the time we reached Neath, including lads from Bridgend, Port Talbot as well as The I.V.F. and with the Neath lads joining us there were twenty three cars speeding towards Swansea.

We parked by The Cricketers Arms and made our way by foot through the side streets until we arrived at the Court House. There were about ninety of us and as I scanned their faces I thought we had a good tight firm, I had stood side by side with many of them in the past, there was an air of confidence that oozed from us. Looking down across the green to the streets below we could see a mob of Jacks approaching, with about the same numbers, they made their way across the green towards us. At this point our firm split, with half charging towards the Jacks and the rest of us standing at the Court House, this caused loads of confusion with lads shouting to stick together and for the lads who were by now halfway across the green to rejoin us. The lads stopped running and returned to the Court House, I don't know what the Jacks thought of this; one minute there were forty lads running at them and then suddenly they stop and run back up the hill, I believe that gave the Jacks confidence and they thought Cardiff were on the run.

The Jacks kept coming up the hill, throwing stones and rocks, a couple of Bridgend lads were hit on the head and fell to the floor, some of the younger lads started to back off, the rest of us spread out, the usual stance hands out stretched calling them on. They faced us, equal numbers, but instead of a mass charge lads paired off into one on ones, a couple of Neath lads were first up and a couple of lads from Port Talbot were quick to follow.

These early exchanges were won by the Jacks, one of the Neath lads was put on the floor by a couple of heavy punches, I was now expecting us to pile in but everybody stood rooted to the spot. It got worse, another one of our lads went down this was beyond a joke but still no one moved forward, I was now screaming at Keith and Rees to join me and get stuck into the Jacks but they just looked on horrified, I took two steps forward but seeing I was alone I took three steps back. The Jacks had the upper hand this time, there were many lads with us whose arses went, they had no fight in them, their heart wasn't in the job at hand and as the Jack Army advanced we turned and legged it leaving the Neath lads to the mercy of the Jacks.

We were chased through the streets passed The Cricketers Arms, with the Jacks in hot pursuit, lads were diving into their cars and speeding off in every direction, we were now a firm on the run and we had split apart, I was with Keith, Rees and Adie and we had to park our getaway car by the train station and had to keep our wits about us as we made our way to the Vetch. After the game we stopped off in Port Talbot at a pub known as The Scare and enjoyed the hospitality of the lads from The Pure Violence Mob. There was an inquest into what went wrong that day, personally I thought some of the lads had thought the Jacks would be pushovers, the lesson learned was that disrespect any firm at your peril. There were too many lads not up for the fight, some I've never seen again and others I no longer respect and no longer speak to.

The F.A. Cup 1991

The F.A. Cup is always a special competition where teams like Cardiff City have the chance of coming up against bigger teams and better firms, but in 1991, when we were drawn away to Swansea City for most of the lads it was a dream come true.

It was the first time we had played each other on a Saturday afternoon for donkey's ears; all the lads had nonsense planned. I travelled down by train with Turkey and Oz even though we knew the Old Bill would be out in force, we made our way to the ground in a snaking escort it was a wet winters day, and the journey to the ground itself was uneventful. We were herded into the visiting section which was already packed with 3,000 Cardiff fans, and as usual the atmosphere was electric you could feel the hatred on both sides.

Just after kick off fighting broke out in the Central Stand about fifty Neath lads had infiltrated the Jacks, boots and punches were flying in, there were winners and losers on both sides and as the fighting spilled onto the pitch the referee took the both teams off. Unfortunately for us, the game restarted and the Jacks went into a 2-1 lead, the game was coming to a close and the mood started to turn ugly, Paul Perry, Rees, Foster and I went to the back of the stand and to our surprise the main gates were open, we didn't need a second invitation and slipped out into the darkness and around to the North Bank. The Jacks had started streaming out into the street in ones and twos, suddenly Rees was straight into a group of them, boots and fists flailing everywhere, by the time we arrived he had already put one Jack on his arse, we steamed into his mates, they were confused in the darkness as our punches connected with our targets. It had to be a hit and run raid and as we backed off, out of nowhere came a Jack with a pair of nunchukers flying around his head, we stopped and fronted him, then suddenly Paul Perry launched himself at him and brought him to the floor, we were quick to his assistance and gave the Jack a good shoeing, more and more Jacks were arriving on the scene, it was time to fuck off and we managed to get back to the safety of the Away End.

The game had ended by now and the Cardiff fans were streaming towards the parked Double Decker buses laid on to take them back to the train station, I was having none of that I wanted more nonsense. I grabbed Turkey and we headed back towards the North Bank, we mingled with the Jacks leaving the ground. We made our way to The Swansea Jack pub with a group of about forty lads, outside the boozer were about another 200 lads, this was their firm, they filled the road, Turkey an I kept our mouths shut. All eyes were on the group advancing towards us, "Here they come", the Jacks were saying, as the Cardiff got nearer I could see they had a mob of 400 and worse there were no Old Bill with them. The Jacks sussed this too and as panic started to set in shouts of "Stay!" and "Stick Together!" were the norm, I tugged at Turkey's arm, "We're going to have it by here", I said panicking; I thought we were going to get battered by The Soul Crew; oh the sweet irony. Luckily it didn't come to that, as the Cardiff hordes drew near the Jacks legged it with Turkey and I amongst them we thought that was the safest bet. We made our way behind a multi storey car park, the Jacks had scattered, and there were only remnants of their firm left. Turkey and I stopped for a breather, with us was a podgy Jack kitted out in a white Armani sweatshirt, the fat bastard was knackered he panted "That was fucking lucky, I thought those Cardiff cunts had us for sure", a large smile cracked across his face, Turkey soon wiped that off with a right-hander to the jaw that knocked the Jack into the road, "Lets fuck off", said Turkey, well said I thought.

We made our way back towards the Quadrant and the main shopping centre and took our rightful place within the marauding Cardiff mob. No one seemed to know where we were going, we just wandered aimlessly through the deserted city streets, until a large mob was spotted at the top of the street, we moved as one gaining pace as we walked towards them, they had about the same numbers and were hell bent on violence, they quickly moved towards us. The two mobs met head on and as we did I could see familiar faces, these were Cardiff, what's more we were all Cardiff. We moved on an army of 800 Soul Crew, along the Kingsway we went and outside Martha's nightclub stood 200 Jacks, their firm had regrouped and once again they filled the road. Without hesitation we steamed into them scattering them everywhere, most of their firm disintegrated but those who stood took a hell of a beating, the police had lost control and law and order had totally broken down. We were free to do what we pleased, we held the city to ransom, some lads were looting shops, others overturned cars and numerous windows were put through, it was carnage and we destroyed everything and everyone in our path as we slowly made our way back to the train station.

The Welsh press had a field day and once again the Soul Crew were depicted as animals and scum.

Rob's Stag Night

It was not only at the footy we clashed, the bitter hatred spilt over anywhere, and many times my mates and I had came unstuck on nights out in Swansea, once they had sussed you nonsense was guaranteed and for this reason birthdays and stag nights had to be celebrated in Swansea.

Rob's stag night was to be no exception; a 40-seater coach and a 17-seater minibus were duly hired. We were picked up outside the Brownhills Hotel in Cardiff, Rob had invited some family and friends along, these were non-footy people, but the rest were hardcore terrace violence, in total there were 40 Soul Crew in attendance, all decked out in Aquascutum blazers, Farah slacks or chinos.

We arrived in Swansea city centre at 7 O'clock and our first port of call was The Terminus after a swift pint and a quick tour of the city centre bars and it was onto The Queens, the Jack's main boozer, we entered the bar, it was packed, the Jacks were having a Karaoke party. We got a couple of pints in at the bar made ourselves known and took a backseat and waited for the fireworks, we waited and waited but nothing happened, the Jacks didn't fancy it and a couple of Cardiff chants later we were asked to leave.

Time was racing along and we started to split up, groups of threes and fours drifted away into Chinese Restaurants and Curry Houses, the main group of us headed for The Aviary nightclub, we were down to about twenty of us by now. A couple of pints later and I could see the Jacks mobbing up, news had spread and they were feeling a lot braver now. Inevitably one of our boys got jumped in the toilets and then scuffles broke out on the dance floor, the place was packed and you couldn't tell where the next attack was going to come from. Suddenly, all hell broke loose, we were engulfed by Jacks and doormen, I lashed out indiscriminately hitting anyone within my reach, we were being forced towards the stairs and our numbers were getting smaller and smaller as one after another of us were thrown unceremoniously down the thirty or so stairs. I thought fuck this and made my own way down the stairs, while bodies came flying passed me, once outside we regrouped, a bit battered and bruised and a few worse for wear, the Old Bill were soon on the scene trying to sort everything out, but a couple of Rob's family and friends had been involved and one of them was seriously hurt with a back injury sustained when he was thrown down the stairs. Rob was going mental and was trying to get back in the club to sort the Jacks out, but all he managed to do was to get himself nicked, and he would play no further part in the action. The Old Bill moved us on further down the road, where Moody recognised a known face in the Jack firm, Moody was straight in, dragging him into a nearby car park, the Jack lad didn't want to know and managed to wriggle himself free and sped off.

We had two hours left before our coaches arrived and with our numbers diminishing every Jack in the city wanted a piece of us and it wasn't long before we bumped into a mob of their lot, the numbers were even as we both attacked each other Mark H was straight in, using his power and muscle to good effect, scattering all-comers. Moody piled into a fat bloke sending him to his knees, we were unstoppable and backed them off down the road. Running battles carried on throughout the next couple of hours, with both mobs scoring minor victories off each other. One major altercation saw the Jacks regroup and come at us, one waving a whole length of exhaust pipe above his head, Mark H made straight for him but was smashed across his head leaving him clearly stunned; we ran to back him up, Rees and I soon had the Jack down and disarmed, scuffles and skirmishes were going off all across the road, the Jacks numbers grew as more pubs emptied and they started to back us off down the road, the police stood by and watched us take a beating, as if they wanted us to be taught a lesson. The Jacks ran us ragged for the last fifteen minutes until our coaches arrived.

The Old Bill finally intervened and we all clamoured onto our coaches and the Jacks were dispersed. As I sank into the seat, I was physically drained, my arms were like lead, I ached from head to toe, my face was so sore all I wanted to do was sleep, I felt I had gone ten rounds with Mike Tyson, as I looked around the empty seats of the coach it suddenly dawned on me that half the lads had either been hospitalised or nicked, that was the hardest night of my life.

The Jacks have a good tight mob and are very rarely done at home and some English firms rate Swansea higher than Cardiff, with plenty of them coming unstuck in the many back streets around the Vetch. The Jacks don't travel well though and have never troubled us at Ninian Park; plus they don't follow Wales in large numbers either, I don't know whether its because they're not very patriotic or whether they're wary of being slapped by The Soul Crew but whatever their reasons they tend to stay at home on International days.

The Play-Off Final 2005/06

Now to events closer to the present day; the 2005/06 Season was quite successful for our neighbours. They won the Football Association of Wales Cup as well as appearing at the Millennium Stadium on two occasions; the first to lift the LDV Vans Trophy and secondly and more importantly the League One Play-Off Final against Barnsley. Swansea had led the Division for long periods and should have clinched automatic promotion but a dip in form around Christmas and again in the latter stages of the Season meant they had to take their chances in the lottery that is the Play-Offs.

This was a big game for our firm and there were plenty of us who wanted to get revenge on the Jacks; recently they had carried out a couple of sneaky attacks on Cardiff. Latterly, The Jacks had begun to stop off in Cardiff on their way home from away games, they would enter a city centre boozer give a few "Jack Army's", slap a couple of locals and fuck off back on the train. Normally, the people they attacked were innocent drinkers or lads in Cardiff shirts, all a bit out of order I think.

On the day of the Final the Jacks brought an army of around 25,000 supporters who descended on Cardiff for their biggest game in years. I personally was rooting for the Jacks because I believe the higher the Welsh clubs can progress in the football league it will ultimately benefit our National team and Welsh football in general.

As always with matches played at the Millennium Stadium the Old Bill ensure we don't mob up in the city centre, so the majority of our lads were plotted up in Canton while others mobbed up in boozers on the outskirts of the city centre; although you also get a dozen or so of our lot fringing around the packed city centre pubs and I was one of them.

It was a horrible grey day and the rain lashed down onto the packed Cardiff streets. Swansea's supporters were allocated the Southern half of the city and their Firm were packed into the Prince of Wales and the Mill Lane Café Quarter. The bulk of their Firm sheltered under the canopies in Mill Lane they had about 300 lads most of their older heads were out for this one; they looked a tasty outfit.

Barnsley were in the Northern half of the city and what I saw of them they didn't have much of a Firm out and they didn't seem a match for the Jacks but with the number of police on duty a major off was never on the cards.

The trouble that did occur took place on the outskirts of the city; most Firms know that the Soul Crew plot up in Canton and the Jacks are no different and small groups of their lot came looking and duly came unstuck when they came up against equal numbers; both mobs clashed at the

Junction outside the Westgate pub; our lot were straight into them, they smashed their way through their front line and the Jack's resistance disintegrated and they made a dash for the safety of their minibuses with our lot in hot pursuit; as the minibuses pulled off they came under a hail of rocks and most of the windows were put through the driver roared off with the Jacks cowering under the seats.

Violence also erupted during the game as a group of ticket less Jacks from Den Haag in Holland drank in the Cayo but also present were a group of our lot. Once the Jacks lost the match on penalties the Jacks kicked off but once again they had bitten off more than they had bargained for and one of the Dutch lads had a pint glass shoved in his mush; I won't name the lads involved in these incidents because the Old Bill are still trying to trace them.

After the match the majority of Swansea supporters immediately headed back west, while others chose to drown their sorrows for a couple of hours in boozers around the Stadium. At around 8 o'clock the Old Bill wanted to clear the Jacks from the city but the 300 hardcore had other ideas and they kicked it off with the Old Bill outside the Prince of Wales but after about fifteen minutes the Old Bill managed to force them back on the trains and back to Swansea.

CHAPTER FIVE

DEFENDING OUR MANOR

Valley Life

In the mid eighties I had become friendly with a group of lads from Hopkinstown near Pontypridd and we had started drinking at the Champions Bar in the precinct at Pontypridd, this was a new Sportsman Bar and was proving very popular; people travelled from Rhydyfelin, Llantwit Fadre, Ynysybwl, and other local villages plus the Rhondda and Cynon valleys. The Valleys were grey and deprived and full of hard men; I've seen a full-scale brawl kick-off over a spilt drink. There were hard men in all the pubs some were full-on villains; luckily they chose to remain in their on circles while we stayed in ours and although our paths never crossed there was a mutual respect between the two groups.

Pontypridd was a very busy market town and a gateway to the Rhondda, Cynon and Merthyr Valleys and was always a melting pot with gangs of lads from the above towns descending on us every weekend. There was always a simmering tension underneath the surface and Fridays and Saturdays were always tense affairs littered with plenty of gang fights spilling out onto the busy streets from the packed boozers and The Champions Bar was no exception.

Every Friday, Saturday and Sunday we could be found in the Champions Bar, this was our local, and on several occasions we were forced to defend it. Normally, we had twenty lads on hand including Bitten, Oz, Turkey, Dai "Morphine" Morgan, Dean Thomas, Ashley, Karl "Monster" Fletcher, Dyllis, Jason, Cen, Dava the Scouse, Dukey, Johnny Edmonds and myself as well as some local lads who had no interest in the footy. We were a tight mob and always looked out for each other.

On one occasion a mob of Rhydyfelin lads had bowled up and started gobbing off, and spouting threats towards us. It was early doors on a Saturday evening and the boozer was quite empty and it was obvious that they had been on the booze all day, these were hard lads but were not in our league, we were used to mob violence through our escapades with The Soul Crew. After plotting our attack, Bitten was first to front them and planted a left hook on a tall ginger lad, that was our cue Dava, Ashley, Cen and myself were immediately at Bitten's shoulder, they didn't know what had hit them and by the time the rest of our lads had steamed in there were four lads sprawled on the floor and another half dozen were being beaten out the door, after we had seen them off, Bitten walked over to the ginger lad who was trying desperately to get to his knees and put one of the wrought iron tables over his head and rendered him unconscious. The other three lads slowly got to their feet and carried ginger outside. Once outside they sat ginger on one of the many plastic chairs and waited until he came around.

Soon the local plod were on the scene, and the Rhydyfelin lads suddenly grew braver and started to gob off through the windows and gave us the finger, the Old Bill swiftly moved in and started to escort them from the precinct but we were already out the door and we charged through the Old Bill, once again Bitten was first in, and nailed ginger again, Dava and I were next swapping blows with their lads, they were now on their toes and so were we with the Old Bill in pursuit, but we ducked up one of the many side streets and we were away.

Pontypridd at this time was a moody town and you never knew when you might be attacked, and like most valley towns everyone knew each other so if you upset someone you could bet that they would come looking for you sooner rather than later. One Saturday night we had left the Champions Bar and headed for Gingers, a very popular nightclub at the time, Oz and Dean Thomas left us to get some food from a burger van. While they were queuing two lads from Llantwit Fadre attacked them, Oz was kicked in the bollocks and Dean took a slap to the head. This was totally unprovoked and well out of order.

We caught up with their attackers in Taff Street, we crossed the street into them, once again Bitten was first in, followed by Dean both throwing a flurry of punches, these blokes were big and weren't going down too easily, Oz and I steamed in and we managed to get the big blonde bloke on the ground and we set on him like rabid animals kicking and stamping on his head, we showed no mercy, and when we were finished he was left with his shirt ripped off his back lying in a pool of blood. This was different from the footy this was personal.

We walked away feeling pretty pleased with ourselves, but we knew that would not be the last we'd see of them.

We didn't have to wait long, the following weekend, as we left the Champions Bar and made our way out of the precinct a punch came out of nowhere and caught Oz right on the button, he dropped to the floor like a lead balloon, he crumpled unconscious in a heap, when we looked around there was the blonde bloke from Llantwit Fadre, we picked Oz up and for this once we left it like that. This bloke was a thorn in Oz's side, and we found out later he was also a Cardiff fan.

A fortnight later, another busy Friday night in the Champions Bar, and once again Blondie was there but this time he was mobbed up, there were around twenty of them including five Glasgow Rangers lads whom they had met on holiday and were obviously playing up to impress them. We only had eleven out, including Bitten, Oz, Dean and myself, and we knew there was going to be some nonsense later.

First to approach us was Blondie's younger brother who was later joined by one of the Jocks, and after they had finished with their threats they both tapped their jacket pockets, as if to imply they were carrying blades, this would be quite common at this time with the favoured weapon being the Stanley knife, and to be honest we weren't strangers to tooling ourselves up either.

Closing time came in a flash and as we left the Bar, Blondie and his lads mobbed up behind us and followed us out, we were largely outnumbered and the seven normal lads weren't up for it, so then there were four. We left the precinct and crossed the road, I said to Bitten, "Stand firm, keep it tight", he smiled, their lads were now stood opposite us, and spread out across the pavement, I looked at Bitten, "Lets 'ave it!" he screamed and we were off into them, I charged towards Blondie's brother, I landed a couple of blows to his head, then Bitten shouted, "Goughy, run", and as I turned Bitten was backing away and Blondie was staggering around and you couldn't see his face for blood, I ran passed him and grabbed Oz, "C'mon lets get out of 'ere", Dean and Oz joined us as we made our getaway up the hill by the Y.M.C.A. the Llantwit lads had now split into two groups some stayed with their stricken mate while the rest ran after us. Coming down the hill were our seven mates, so we stopped running turned and steamed straight back into them. I felt a tug on my jacket it was Bitten, "Mike we've got to fuck off", I looked at him puzzled but did has he said, from the top of the hill I could see Oz and Dean still in the thick of the action, Oz was belt whipping a lad on the floor and Dean had put one of the Jocks on his arse. Bitten and I fled the scene, "I've been cut", Bitten said and I could see a gaping hole in his hand, we made our way to a mates house who bandaged him up.

Bitten and I made our way home and arranged to meet the following day. I called at Bitten's around 6:30pm to be told by his mother the Old Bill had picked him up. I was to learn later that Blondie had been slashed and had undergone surgery to have over 100 stitches put in his face and neck, and also, all the lads including Oz and Dean had also been lifted, I knew it wouldn't be long before I would be picked up too.

Sunday afternoon I was at home watching Highway to Heaven when there was a knock on the door, two burly blokes in bad suits, "Are you Mr. Michael Gough?" they asked, I nodded, "May we come in?" they flashed their C.I.D. warrant cards, I led them into the lounge where the rest of my family were sat, one told my father of the trouble in Pontypridd on the weekend while the other rifled through my wardrobe and laundry basket, they found my bloodstained jeans and Burberry Golfer and kept them for forensic tests. They then informed my father I was helping them with their enquiries and I was taken to Pontypridd police station.

Once at the station I was shown photographs of Blondie, his face was in a right state, they accused me and threatened to charge me with Malicious Wounding with Intent, they interrogated me for a couple of hours then released me without charge. Bitten and Oz weren't so lucky they were held over the weekend and appeared at a special court on Monday morning both jointly charged with Malicious Wounding with Intent to endanger life, which if found guilty would carry a sentence of five years in the big house. They were both put on curfews awaiting the trial and had to report to Pontypridd police station every Friday and Saturday evening so we didn't see much of them at the footy for a while.

Eight months later the trial began at Cardiff Crown Court, Oz had been acquitted a couple of weeks previous with all charges dropped, so Bitten stood alone in the dock reading the Sporting Life as the trial unfolded around him. Witness after witness took their turn on the stand all for the prosecution, I was the only defence witness, I gave my evidence and returned to the gallery, the victim was up next, he stared hard at Bitten, his wounds had healed but he still had terrible scars, scars that will be a constant reminder of that night.

He gave his evidence, and like everyone before him he could not identify Bitten as the person who slashed him. The judge summed up the case and he instructed the jury to find Bitten not guilty because all the evidence the Old Bill had was circumstantial. The Old Bill ushered us out of court and we never saw Blondie in Pontypridd again.

The Hardest Battle

When I talk about defending your manor it's not just about local boozers, your home town or your footy club its more far reaching than that, it's about defending your way of life, your culture and your livelihoods.

Just over twenty years ago one of the biggest pitched battles of the industrial revolution took place. The battle of Orgreave took place in May 1984 during the bitter Miner's strike. Growing up in the Rhondda valley the coal industry always played a huge part in the community. The coalfield itself consisted of five mines and was the biggest employer of the region, so the strike affected everyone, even those not employed in the mines.

Before the strike the Rhondda valley enjoyed a vibrant economy and the local pubs we frequented were always full of hardworking miners relaxing, the pubs were full of larger than life characters and there was never a dull moment. These men were not only our mates but were the heartbeat of the community.

The strike started on the 6th March 1984, when the head of the National Coal Board, Ian McGregor, announced plans to cut production at 20 pits or the equivalent of 20,000 jobs. Many were to be in Wales and were seen by many as, "The Rape of the Green Country", and the beginning of the end of coalmining in the Rhondda valley. Most men felt a sense of betrayal after many years loyal service and many were filled with anger as well as being worried about their immediate futures.

Many miners from the area were travelling by coach to Orgreave coking plant near Sheffield as part of Arthur Scargill's Flying Pickets. A couple of mates and I had decided to lend our support and travel to Orgreave by train; my father worked in heavy industry and was always a strong union man, who believed strongly in righting injustices and better workers rights, he was very political and I was brought up with strict left wing and socialist beliefs and principles, plus our mate Keith was a miner, so we wanted to show him our support.

We were all in our early twenties and at the time Persil was carrying out a promotion, that involved saving tokens for reduced train fares, we had travelled the length and breadth of the British Isles doing this and coupled with the way we looked, with neat wedge haircuts, rich coloured designer sports tops, stone-washed jeans that were split at the hems and bright white trainers, to the non footy blokes of Porth we were known as the Persil Boys.

The first train out of Cardiff Central left at 5:00am. The sun was just rising as we pulled out of the station, Cen, Johnny and I, all decked out in all our finery, Armani jumpers and Lacoste Polo shirts.

We had all booked time off work; I was working as a Bar Manager at the Polytechnic of Wales at the time, Jon was still at Dental College, training to join the family practice while Cen was a self employed plasterer, so he gave himself the day off. We all enjoyed "the day out", it always broke up the tedium of the 9 to 5, and thanks to Persil we found ourselves having our "away days" more often, but this was our first trip to a picket line. We had heard the usual stories about police brutality, but we wanted to see for ourselves. We neared Sheffield, and as we peered out at the sprawling city skyline, Cen muttered, "It's grim up North innit", it was a cold and stark city, full of grey built up flats, it was a smog filled industrialised area with very little greenery on show. We rose from our seats as we rolled into the bustling station, full of commuters; we left the station and made our way up the hill and the short distance to Orgreave.

We arrived at Orgreave at 8.30am, "Fucking hell, look at this lot", said Johnny, there must have been around 5,000 miners gathered together forming the biggest picket line of the strike so far, flanked by Police Officers from all the surrounding ten counties. All decked out in riot gear and riot shields and all their protective padding made them look very cumbersome. Staring into the faces of the swollen ranks of the local plod I could see that the younger officers were nervous as they fidgeted with their equipment, while the older officers were battle hardened and just gave the miners a hard cold stare, they looked as if they were well up for it.

We took our place on the line and whilst walking through the sea of bodies we quickly noticed that there were not just miners making up the numbers. There were the usual scruff bags of the loony left in the form of The Socialist Workers, who were always up for a row. There were football hooligan firms from Barnsley, Leeds, Sheffield and Rotherham. There were political types like members of the Communist Party plus us three, who were there on the mooch. We had all gathered together united in trying to prevent the haulage lorries from stocking up their load, initially the mood was strained but jovial, with good natured banter flying from both sides, this was all to change when the first of the lorries heading the convoy roared into sight at around 9.00am, which led to an almighty surge forward into the police lines knocking police helmets into the road. Huge cheers from miners standing away from the melee greeted this. The miners at the rear kept surging forward and we were caught in the middle, I was lifted off the floor by the unrelenting pressure. The police in the front were battling to keep the road open with shouts of, "Hold the line!" as the lorries roared down the road. The miners and police alike were jostling each other and batons were drawn to beat the miners back, this was met with a flurry of punches, and from the back of the crowd came a hail of stones and bottles that rained down on their own as well as their intended targets. The jostling and fighting carried on, the ferocity astounded us, the noise was deafening, and the police were beating their shields in defiance and stood firm. They faced wave after wave of brutal attacks but the miners could not penetrate the police line and the convoy of lorries safely entered the factory gates.

There was now a standoff and during this respite I saw a lot of bloodied miners with heads cracked open, exhausted and bewildered men, most of whom were law abiding citizens, some not believing the kind of beatings being meted out by the police. My friends and I had seen this all too often at football grounds up and down the country. With the use of police spotters, the police took this opportunity to use snatch squads to infiltrate the throng of tired pickets. They grabbed the ringleaders or known faces, normally union men, and dragged them to awaiting police vans, where they were held before being arrested and appearing in local magistrates courts.

The miners had failed to prevent the lorries entering the plant, and there were some very dejected and deflated men, it was at this moment Scargill walked amongst his men trying to gee them up with impromptu speeches and rallying calls, urging his men to stand tall and prevent the lorries leaving. We made our way through the line. Our once pristine clothes were now drenched in sweat and Johnny's polo shirt had a large rip in it, this delighted Cen, because he knew how much Jon, like us loved his clothes. We walked around the encampment and saw plenty of battered miners who were regrouping, readying themselves for the next assault, and trying to find things to arm themselves with. The time seemed to drag while we all stood around waiting for the heavy convoy of lorries to depart. We strolled around behind the police line trying to kill time. We saw friends tending each other's wounds, once they worked shoulder to shoulder now they fought shoulder to shoulder, fighting to keep their pits open and to provide employment for future generations. It was at this moment an uneasiness descended and the whole mood changed, neither side trusted each other, there were even rumours that some of the police were actually Army personnel planted by Thatcher just to stir things up.

However, there were still some sections of the massed picket line that seemed to have a good rapport with the police, and there were some officers who sympathised with the miners but they were a tiny minority. Within most sections there was an ominous undercurrent and I sensed it was only a matter of time before it kicked off again. The police weren't helping matters by flashing their payslips showing the amount of overtime they were working, while the miners themselves were unable to get any financial assistance and soup kitchens had been starting up in many mining communities.

Suddenly, there was uneasiness within the ranks of the police and I noticed worried faces through their protective visors, they hurriedly readjusted their protective gear and the news started filtering throughout the massed ranks of pickets that the lorries were about to leave, everybody started to regroup and jostle the police. Once again there came a hail of stones, bottles, pieces of wood, smoke bombs and ball bearings, raining down on the hundreds of police trying to keep the peace. The police retaliated by drawing their truncheons and hitting out indiscriminately at anyone within arms length, sending men of all shapes and sizes reeling backwards. I looked around and saw fear filled faces, many of whom had never been in this situation, they seemed to be caught in the wrong place at the wrong time, and as they fled attempting to find safety, the gaps they had created were plugged and the picket line would quickly regroup and charge again at the police. There were some successes, when injured officers would be dragged from the line leaving a gap for the miners to attack.

In the mayhem the lorries filled with their prized black gold careered off down the road with screams of "Scab! Scab! Scab!" ringing in the drivers' ears, bricks and bottles bouncing off the sides of their cabs. The miners knew this was their last chance and another almighty surge came from the back, men of all sizes pushing and shoving from all angles, crushing everyone at the front, and I felt the life being sucked out of my lungs. I was forced up against the cold riot shields, I stared right into the visor of my adversary, fear etched on both our faces, I was trying to catch my breath, I somehow found the strength and pushed myself away from the crush, turning I looked for my mates, I saw their reddened faces struggling in the crowd. Cen was smiling manically and loving every minute. He and Johnny were right in the thick of it, neither of them were adverse to a bit of fisticuffs and were pushing to and fro, but once again the police pushed back using riot shields and truncheons to beat the hordes back. I looked around and saw hundreds of contorted faces and straining heaving bodies moving as one, like a vast machine surging forward but being pushed back by the unyielding blue line.

Suddenly, there was a break in the picket line and the police used this opportunity to force us back, as we fled we were chased and beaten by the heavy handed storm troopers, I saw miners strewn around the gravel floor bleeding from gaping head wounds and ambulance men wearing protective headgear leading casualties away to safety. The police had gained the upper hand and the picket line was broken, the miners were in disarray, it was like a battlefield with miners and police going toe to toe, there were miners being beaten on the floor by baton wielding thugs, also on the other hand there were groups of miners clad in N.C.B. and N.U.M. donkey jackets administering a kicking to officers who had became isolated from their units, it seemed everyone was fair game and personally I found this whole experience an extreme adrenalin rush, I was bouncing.

It was at this point the police played their Trump card and sent in the horses. The miners were already fleeing and the horses made it easier for the police to divide and conquer. I've never liked the use of police on horseback; my mates and I had come up against this attack many times, especially when dealing with the South Yorkshire Constabulary. The horses charged, targeting the troublemaking element, which they saw as orchestrators. Initially the beleaguered miners tried to stand their ground, some even managed to pull a couple of officers from their mounts and these were given a good shoeing by the baying crowd, but the pockets of resistance were getting smaller. With the sun beating down on us we grew wearier with every horse led assault, the police were deliberately riding into us and self-preservation was foremost in our minds. In our panic we were trampling on fallen comrades, men soaked in blood drenched t-shirts, with blood streaming down their faces from open wounds, the horses were after us getting closer by the minute, I could feel its hot breath on the back of my neck I didn't dare look round, the thought of a truncheon over the head was daunting enough but personally I feared getting nicked, and that would have been the end of my job for sure, a sudden change of direction and I'm free from its attention. Our numbers were falling and we were all losing the energy to fight, sensing victory the foot soldiers took over, charging into us knocking fatigued bodies to the ground, we desperately clambered out of their way but were eventually rounded up and penned in. We were battered, bruised and exhausted and finally peace was restored. The police slowly escorted us away from the factory. Walking within the mass of miners the three of us huddled together and this was the first time I noticed that Cen's smile had left him and was replaced with a look of shock. It had been a hard day.

After the battle there were 41 police officers and 28 miners injured. During the fierce clashes that lasted for most of the day, the police made 81 arrests. The 34 lorry drivers managed to make two journeys into the Orgreave coking plant unhindered, and said they were determined to continue the coke runs. In the aftermath both sides tried to blame each other Scargill said, "The intimidation and the brutality that has been displayed are something reminiscent of a Latin American state", while South Yorkshire Chief Constable Peter Wright said, "My officers had to wear protective helmets and use shields to allow the gates of the factory to remain open".

This was just one of many defeats the miners suffered in what was a long bloody dispute that split and shattered many mining communities throughout Britain. Thatcher and her Conservative government would not be defeated and had a concerted plan of action; a National Reporting Centre was set up to co-ordinate Britain's regional police force. This allowed officers to be deployed quickly to trouble spots to tackle Scargill's flying pickets that he had sent all over the country to persuade workers to down tools. The pickets had very little success however and failed to stop the power supply of the country. They also failed to get the much-needed support of other unions. We never took our place on the picket line again, but we helped out amongst the community as much as we could and we ensured that none of our mates went without food or a night out.

The strike ended in March 1985. The broken but unbowed miners of Maerdy Colliery in the Rhondda were the last to return to work. Once again my mates and I were there to show our support and at 5.30am on a cold misty morning the whole community marched through the colliery gates with a full brass band leading the way.

There are now no working mines in the Rhondda valley and unemployment stands at 25% of the community. The Rhondda valley is a shell of its former self. Where once there were green mountains and fields these have been replaced by a dull Rhondda Grey, it's a dirty grim hellhole of a place where drug and alcohol abuse is rife. Heroin overdoses are a daily occurrence, and those who seek a prosperous future do so outside the valley, whether going to English universities or commuting daily to work in Cardiff. The Rhondda valley has nothing to offer most of its residents and nothing for the three of us who left Porth in May 1984. Cen now lives in London; Johnny lives in Barry, while I have found employment in Cardiff.

CHAPTER SIX

SIX OF THE BEST

I have been involved in quite a few Terrace wars over the decades, certainly too many to recount but here are some that stick out in my memory the most, in no particular order and for no particular reason.

Hull City Away

Our next fixture was Hull City away and this was a must for us, Hull were very much like Cardiff; a shit team amidst a heavily industrialised area that were followed by working class lads. A couple of the lads had been to Hull with Chelsea in the Cup and had been really impressed with the mob they turned out, they were well up for it and gave Chelsea a lot of problems.

The minibus was booked, the lads of the I.V.F. and I set off on the long journey north. We were travelling by road more frequently now, train prices had soared and with Cardiff City in decline on the pitch the number of lads travelling had dwindled.

We had travelled together on numerous occasions, we had been together since 1982 and the start of the Soul Crew; I classed these lads as by best mates and I knew that they all could be relied on if it turned nasty, which it usually did; we had a strange knack of finding trouble.

There were fifteen of us, including Pennall, Dean Greatrex and Turkey plus of course the usual suspects, we had a nice little number, not too many to draw attention to ourselves but enough to do the business. We were travelling in luxury, the minibus actually had seats, we normally travelled the country in the back of transit vans sitting on mattresses and jackets.

We made good time, the Motorways were quiet and we wiled away the time enjoying plenty of booze and Class A's. We arrived at Hull just after midday and headed straight for the Fiveways Pub, which was just a short walk from the ground, most of us were already bladdered as we left the minibus.

We left The Fiveways around 2:30 and made our way to the ground, we were all bladdered by now and I was finding it increasingly difficult to walk and I was glad to see the stadium up ahead. We lurched into the car park and there were hundreds of people milling around, we made our way through the crowd and tried to locate the Visitors End, we must have stood out like sore thumbs, and soon there was a mob of a dozen leather clad Northerners making their way towards us, we all stood our ground, most of us were too pissed to run. The Hull made straight for us, Pennall and Turkey lunged forward, both their punches connected and two Hull lay on the ground, the rest of us were a step behind, the Hull backed off a couple of steps. I swung my boot at one of the lads on the ground but to my horror I was so bladdered I fell on top of him, as I wrestled to find my feet he gave me a couple of slaps in the face and finally Turkey pulled me up, the Hull attacked again but got the same response from us and a flurry of punches and boots sent them running backwards, the Old Bill were soon on the scene and in our panic we scattered, running in all directions and in the chaos I tripped over a garden wall and knocked myself out for a minute or so. I staggered to my feet and I was alone, I made my way back towards the ground, I kept my head down as I walked through the car park; paranoia had got hold of me I felt hundreds of unwelcoming eyes on me; pulling the collar of my jacket up to disguise myself I hurriedly headed for the Away End. Once I was safely in the ground I went to sleep at the front of the terracing. The game itself passed me by; I found out later we had lost 4-2 and that Lee Baddeley and Paul Miller had been sent off.

****

I've been to Hull since then; Rogers from Bedwas and I spent the night at Pricey's and what was supposed to be a couple of quiet drinks before our early start turned into a heady cocktail of Alcohol, Class A's, The Pogues and the Anti-Nowhere League which had us buzzing all night. The morning arrived with a vengeance and with very little sleep we stumbled out of Pricey's terraced house. The grey valley town was still cloaked in darkness as we moved slowly down the High Street towards our Battle Bus; once aboard we were greeted by the same usual faces and as we left the valley behind the sun began to rise. The Old Bill were the winners that day; they cancelled two of our battle buses at the last moment, which meant only 70 of us made the trip. We mobbed up in Goole in the boozer opposite the station where we met up with a handful of Jocks but once again the Old Bill put a spanner in the works; they delayed our train so that we didn't get to Hull until 2:30, then they walked us along the longest route to Boothferry Park as possible; which meant we didn't reach the stadium until 3:30. Surprisingly we still came face to face with some Hull outside the ground; these weren't your usual football mob but made up of Loons, Gypos and Nutters from the local council estate. The Old Bill tried to keep us apart but a couple of lads from both sides managed to get a few punches in, as we neared the ground a small group of Hull charged out of their end but they were soon on their toes as we chased them back inside but the stewards managed to close the gates on us. At the final whistle about 500 Hull were mobbed up under a railway bridge but the Old Bill were well on top and no Hull managed to break through the blue line. We were put on our awaiting coach and taken away from the area and that was the end of our day.

****

I've also seen Hull at Ninian Park and they've never disappointed. They visited Cardiff on a Friday night and were very well represented, they brought over a hundred lads, which for an evening game was virtually unheard of.

As they stood on the Grange End I observed them carefully, their firm consisted of a hardcore of lads in their mid thirties and early forties with a few youngsters thrown in, they looked like they meant business. Five minutes before the end a small group of us including Eckhardt, Lakey, Pasti and I left the ground, there were about twenty of us milling around the Away End entrance. At the final whistle the gates opened and both our firms met in the car park opposite, Hull had the larger numbers and made us pay, we both fronted each other; their mob came into us and after a short scuffle they backed us off further up the car park and even though more of us were turning up we couldn't regain the initiative and victory on that occasion was theirs.

Peter, a friend of mine had become friendly with a few of the Hull firm over the years, I've been introduced to a couple of their lads and what I've seen they definitely like the nonsense.

Huddersfield Town Away

It was the 1995/96 Season and another northern adventure for the I.V.F. beckoned, Huddersfield Town away, I'd already been to Huddersfield we had lost 4-0 at Leeds Road in the early Eighties, with Mark Lillis scoring four goals. The Huddersfield had taunted us about the Aberfan disaster all through the game and at the final whistle we broke down the iron gates and spilled into the car park and scattered Huddersfield's mob everywhere.

They were now playing at The McAlpine Stadium a new ground for most of us and once again we travelled by minibus, there were twelve of us venturing north including, Ambler, Kenny Ham, Gabe, Hugh plus the usual bunch who went everywhere and Lakey. This was the first time I met Mr Rivers but had obviously heard of him, he had made a bit of a reputation for himself within certain circles. He was quite a bit younger than most of us and was constantly on his mobile phone, and he was definitely the best dressed amongst us.

Although Lakey refers to this altercation in his book "The Soul Crew", I include this simply because of the sheer backs to the wall defiance shown by the lads in the face of such overwhelming numbers. Also, at the time as the events unfolded I promised myself to remember the events of that day. Out of all the rows I've been apart of this one's a bit special.

Once in Huddersfield, Lakey met a lad he knew and he told us that Huddersfield's firm were mobbed up in the Crescent and for us to give it a wide berth. We headed for the George Hotel instead; where we met Simon's mate Rowan. The Hotel was just a short walk from the Crescent separated only by a busy main road.

After a short while we were joined by two Huddersfield lads, who were obviously sussing us out, they checked our numbers, exchanged small talk, they seemed pissed off by our small numbers and kept banging on about our visit to Bradford a couple of seasons earlier, they looked us up and down and left, but we knew they'd be back.

It wasn't long before a large mob started walking towards our hotel, they spread out across the road opposite, a few of us grabbed stools and went to the front door to prevent them getting in. I was staring at them through the large glass doors, the adrenalin was pumping through me, and I had that nervous feeling in the pit of my stomach, I gripped my stool tighter as about a dozen rushed the door, we moved towards them, they were bouncing, there were lots of taunts and threats of serious injury from the pumped up Northerners but they never made it in, I wasn't too impressed with their mob, what I could see they were a lot younger than us, they seemed all mouth, while with the exception of Lakey we were all in our thirties and had been in this kind of situation on numerous occasions. The manager arrived and locked the door; he was obviously worried for the safety of his guests as well as his Hotel.

The Huddersfield mob had now swollen to about fifty, I thought this is it, this is what we've come here for, I looked around at the lads, Rees, Ambler, Adie and Keith were itching to get out at them. The Old Bill arrived on the scene shortly after, they forced the Huddersfield mob across the road opposite and took Digger our driver to fetch the minibus.

The minibus duly arrived and the two officers escorted us out of the Hotel, as we neared the minibus a couple of Northerners started hurling pool balls at us, which they had brought from the Crescent, we advanced towards them, initially only a handful of us led by Rees, the Northerners rushed towards us safe in the knowledge we were outnumbered but that counted for nothing and Rees was straight into them hurling punches, we were right behind him, the two Old Bill tried desperately to part us but by now all twelve of us were involved this was a full scale row, we were going toe to toe and scuffles were breaking out everywhere outside the Hotel, with the terrified guests peering through the windows.

Boots and fists were flying everywhere, it was toe to toe, but the Huddersfield kept coming, the two Huddersfield lads from the Hotel were right at the front and were game as fuck and we were forced back against the Hotel wall, but we weren't going to be beaten and rallied again and we managed to back the Huddersfield onto the road, one on ones were breaking out all over and a couple of Northerners tried to get behind us, Adie, Simon and myself set about them but after a couple of scuffles it was stalemate with no one giving an inch, Adie tried to hurl a sandwich board at them but to his disgust it was chained to the railings but the Huddersfield got the message and backed off.

The police reinforcements arrived and regained control, and we were put in our minibus but not before chants of "Shit, shit, shit", let them know what we thought of them, we were then escorted to the local nick where we were arrested. Luckily Foster, Hugh and myself were never charged while the others were bound over for a year.

The reason we were so badly represented at Huddersfield was because they had never done anything to earn The Soul Crew's respect, I personally don't remember Huddersfield ever coming to Cardiff with a Firm, and normally you have to either take the piss at Ninian Park or be a team we've got history with, to guarantee a full scale turnout, and Huddersfield don't fall into either category.

Chelsea Home

One team we have plenty of history with is Chelsea; it all began in 1977; Cardiff had gone to Stamford Bridge and wrecked their newly installed electric scoreboard. There's no love lost between the two sets of supporters and every time they've come to Ninian Park there has been trouble and when we played them in the 1983/84 Season it was to be no different. Chelsea were flying high and a swift return to the top flight was on the cards. While Cardiff were in the doldrums and were surely slipping back down to Division Three; at this time we were a yo-yo club, too good for Div 3 yet not good enough for Div 2.

Ashley, Cen and myself set off from Porth nice and early, with the anticipation of seeing a proper firm in action, we were no more than kids in 1983, Ashley was 16, Cen was 18 and I was the eldest at 19, we had only been involved in the scene since 1982 and none of us had seen much action.

We arrived at Cardiff Central station and made our way down the steps of Platform 6 and towards the exit, there in front of us was a massive police presence the like I had never seen at Cardiff. Seeing the numbers of Old Bill it was obvious Chelsea were coming mob handed, it was common knowledge they would travel down by train and the police certainly looked ready for them.

We left the station and headed for the Ninian Park pub, which was just a short distance from the ground, where we knew there would be large numbers of the Soul Crew. The Ninian was packed, both the bar and lounge full of nasty looking blokes. We joined the masses swelling the pavement outside, who seemed to be attacking every van and coach that passed by.

Around midday the three of us made our way to the ground for a nose, we bowled up to the ground entrance by the club's Supporters Shop and there were a handful of coloured lads covered in jewellery. Cardiff have always had a predominately white firm so we knew they weren't our lot. They clocked us immediately and came straight over, they were around the same age as us but like most Cockneys were fucking full of themselves and ripped right into us, they took the piss out of our Burberrys and generally slagged us off, Ashley gave them some verbal back and offered them into the Grandstand; this is where the Soul Crew had started to congregate. They kept on slagging us, calling us gypos, they were so fucking smug that I couldn't help myself, I gave the nearest lad a clout that sent him reeling backwards, this was supposed to be a cue for Ashley and Cen to steam in, but they just stood there. One lad gave Ashley a dig in the ribs that doubled him up, I took a right-hander to the jaw and we were on our toes. I don't know if it was because of the reputation Chelsea had that spooked us, but we were off with our tails between our legs.

We retreated back to the relative safety of the Ninian Park pub, I was gutted that we had run without even putting up a decent fight. We had a couple more pints of Dutch Courage and returned to the ground, and made our way to the Grandstand entrance. There was something different, the usual snaking queue of lads sharing tall tales and the usual banter; was replaced by a subdued orderly line of a dozen or so lads. Unperturbed we joined the line. We paid our money at the turnstile and made our way onto the stand.

We entered the stand itself and made our way passed rows and rows of lads, most of them old heads, we didn't recognise any of them, still we weren't too concerned, we thought they were older top lads who hadn't turned out for a while. We thought they had turned out to have a go at Chelsea. We climbed further up the stand and were glad to see some familiar faces. We took our seats about three rows from the top. There were about 80 of us; our numbers were well down from the normal mob of around 200 that would usually congregate at the top of the stand.

Looking around the ground, Chelsea had filled the Grange End (Visitors Section), the Canton Stand plus both Enclosures; they must have brought around 7,000 with them. We were talking about the amazing away support when the blokes sitting at the bottom of the stand started to chant "Wales! Wales!" and a couple of lads near us joined in, something wasn't right; Cardiff never chanted Wales, other Cardiff lads had sussed it to, I said to Ashley "They're Chelsea", and with a dozen others we made our way down a couple of rows towards them.

The teams came running onto the pitch and 200 blokes rose to their feet in front of us. Gone were the chants of Wales, now it was "Chelsea! Chelsea!" they were in our faces, just a couple of empty rows of seats separated us. They came at us, clambering over the seats. We slowly moved towards them with fists flying, a couple of punches caught me around the head, I could feel my knees go, other Cardiff were jumping over the seats to join us, it was toe to toe but their sheer numbers pushed us back. Some lads tripped over the seats in their panic to get away from Chelsea's marauding mob. Chelsea were advancing up the stand and I could see more Cockneys climbing up from the Enclosure below, I thought at the time "Where's the fucking Old Bill when you need them?" all we could do now was fight, there was nowhere to run and we were slowly battered up the stand and after what seemed like a lifetime the local plod arrived and baton charged the Chelsea back down the stand.

Eighty of us huddled together at the top of the Stand my heart was beating so fast I thought it would burst through my chest, my face reddened from the punches I had received. I looked around at the terrified younger faces sitting around me and I suddenly became aware of Ashley's trembling leg knocking against mine.

"One man went to mow" rang out all around us, we were penned in, surrounded by Chelsea, some of whom were running their fingers across their throats and I personally took that threat very seriously. We sat there nervously as City went 1-0 up, Cardiff always had the knack of doing things you didn't want them to, this just infuriated the Londoners more and spit and coins rained down on us and the police decided it was a good time to escort us out of the Grandstand and onto the Bob Bank

Once on the Bob Bank, we joined 1,000 other City lads, all with tales of personal battles that they had been involved in before kick off, it sounded as if it had been kicking off all over the City, with winners and losers on both sides. On the pitch Cardiff were 3-0 up with ten minutes to go and had surely put a spanner in the works as far as Chelsea's promotion hopes went.

Disgruntled and with violence obviously on their minds, 200 Chelsea lads left the Canton Stand and made their way to the entrance of the Bob Bank. They were looking for a row and we were only too happy to oblige, both sets of lads went toe to toe on the steep hill with only a handful of Old Bill to prevent a full-scale riot. We used our overwhelming numbers to force the Chelsea back down the hill and onto Ninian Park Road, the police battled to restore order and forced us back onto the Bob Bank and closed the large yellow gates, by the time we were all back on the terracing it was 3-2 and in the dying minutes a controversial penalty led to Chelsea's equaliser. Now it was our turn to vent our anger and at the final whistle we steamed out of the ground in pursuit of Chelsea's lads.

We made our way up Ninian Park Road. There were scuffles breaking out everywhere, both on the main road and in the large field opposite Ninian Park. There were Chelsea both in front and behind us and it was almost impossible to tell who was who, there were Old Bill trying to separate the rival mobs, but they had their work cut out and running battles continued up as far as Sloper Road.

Once at the junction the Old Bill pushed us along the main road of Riverside back towards the City centre and the train station, while the 200 Chelsea were escorted towards Canton. The bulk of the Chelsea firm were held under the railway bridge and were forced back towards the ground, while the Old Bill dispersed the hundreds of City lads that had congregated outside the Ninian Park pub.

There were about 300 of us being forced through Riverside when out of one of the many side streets came the 200 Chelsea lads, both mobs met head on and there was a short stand off, then a large Cockney lad dressed in a suede jacket and trademark wedge haircut stepped forward into the road, then a large Skinhead stepped forward from our ranks, unlike Chelsea our mob was made up of Skinheads, Punks and Valley Beer Monsters as well as us dressers of the Soul Crew. The two lads fronted each other and after a short pause got stuck into each other, everyone else just stood and watched; it was surreal for a moment, then we charged. We seemed to catch Chelsea off guard, half their numbers turned and fled the rest were backed off slowly down the side street from where they'd come. On and on we pushed them a number of their lads had been knocked to the ground and were taking a bit of a kicking, then suddenly, they were all running and we were after them. I ran as fast as I could for the chance to get revenge for earlier in the day, this must have clouded my judgement; because while the majority of our lot had given up the chase I was still hot on their heels. I looked around and reality hit me. There was only Prune, myself and a handful of diehards still giving chase, we slowly came to a halt but it was too late Chelsea had now had enough of running and were coming straight at us. I was knackered, but I was also shitting myself. I summoned up all of my energy in a last ditch effort to try and out run the pack of pissed off Londoners who were on my tail. I made it into the main road, but where once 300 lads stood firm now there was a sea of bodies in front of me fleeing the scene. I was getting tired and I could here the dreaded sound of footsteps behind me getting closer and closer, and then out of the corner of my eye I saw this huge right hand coming my way, my brain said duck, but my fatigued body's reactions were too slow and Crack! A piercing blow to my eye, I tried to keep running, my legs were still moving but instead of forward I was now going sideways, until my legs give out completely and I slumped to the floor. All I could see through my one good eye were feet, an assortment of trainers and I waited for the boot to the head but it never came, instead two Chelsea Lads picked me up and took me back to Cardiff Central station. Whilst on the train home to the Rhondda I could feel the whole carriage staring at me and it wasn't until I reached my destination of Porth and saw my reflection in one of the many shop windows that I realised why. My eye was completely closed, my lips were split and swollen and my face was drained of all colour, I was grey. I looked like the Elephant Man.

Throughout the Eighties and early Nineties along with the I.C.F. of West Ham; Chelsea's firm were the most feared in football. On the occasions they both came to Cardiff and after careful observation I personally thought the difference between the two was West Ham never brought large numbers but what did come were pure quality while Chelsea travelled in their thousands and brought both quality and quantity.

We haven't played Chelsea since the Eighties, although they have come to the Cardiff's Millennium Stadium on numerous occasions for various Cup Finals and although most matches passed off without too much incident there were minor skirmishes and scuffles between the two rival firms.

While West Ham on the other hand have been in the Championship with us for the last two seasons and both matches at Ninian Park were played in midweek on Police advice. The first meeting, West Ham brought a nasty crew of around 150 old heads; they arrived in Cardiff around 11:00 a.m a good eight hours before kick-off and the Old Bill placed them in The Springbok Bar a short walk away from the city centre; this is a bar that the majority of our firm never frequent and not one usually used for away firms.

At around 18:00 our firm was milling around and news had spread of West Ham's whereabouts but the Police had the boozer well covered and apart from a few isolated scuffles before the match the Old Bill came out on top.

The next season and another evening encounter, West Ham's firm was much reduced and a lot younger and this time trouble flared after the game with The Soul Crew ambushing the West Ham escort with bottles and bricks as they made their way through Grangetown outside the Grange Public House. The Police took the brunt of the attack and a few officers were injured; the Old Bill arrested a few of our lads, some at the scene and others from CCTV footage and after a lengthy Court case a few alleged ring leaders were imprisoned for their involvement.

Exeter City Away

During the early to mid Eighties, when Cardiff City were yo-yoing between Divisions 2 and 3 and the Soul Crew was at its height, it was commonplace for a minimum of 200 lads to depart Cardiff Central train station in order to terrorise the smaller league clubs.

The Soul Crew was rampant around this time and not happy with the result of running the majority of firms they encountered, they also left a trail of destruction in their wake, vandalising property, overturning parked cars and the looting of stores was a by-product of this organised violence. The Soul Crew had a few young nutters within their ranks at this time; who saw everyone as fair game and innocent fans inadvertently got hurt; this behaviour was frowned upon by the vast majority of us and it left a bad taste in the mouth.

Whilst Cardiff City trawled the lower divisions, the Soul Crew was like a very large fish in a tiny pool we would turn up mob handed in these sleepy backwaters and take the piss all day, very few firms could live with us, but the few that could included our hated rivals from over the Severn Bridge; Bristol City and Rovers and the Wurzels from the West Country; Plymouth Argyle and Exeter City all these clubs were Anti-Welsh and whenever we played them on their manor you could guarantee all the local hard men would turn out for a spot of Taffy bashing.

It was the beginning of another season and we were still languishing in the basement of the football league and Exeter City away was our next fixture. Ashley, Cen and myself left Porth station on the 7:10 train; there were already a score of lads from Treorchy and Ferndale located in the front carriage; joining us at Pontypridd was Bitten, Oz, Monster, Turkey and Dillys a full crew from the Champions Bar, the first away trip of the season always pulled a good crowd of lads. Arriving at Cardiff Central station we met Andy T from Dinas Powys; and it looked like Lacoste polo shirts and cardigans were the order of the day. We made our way to Platform 1 where we joined lads from Neath, Bridgend, and the Pure Violence Mob from Port Talbot as well as a large contingent of Cardiff lads, over 250 lads heading to Wurzelville.

By the time we reached Exeter St. David's we had lost half of our number; over a hundred lads chose to disembark at Taunton in search of cheap Scrumpy and a spot of bovver with the unsuspecting locals. The rest of us were met by a small number of local plod whose intentions were to escort us to the ground, with three hours still to kick-off we had other ideas. The nine of us ducked down the nearest side street in search of a couple of beers and Wurzels.

We found plenty of boozers all rammed with Cardiff; the city centre pubs were awash with Taffies around 500 of us basking in the glorious Summer sunshine. The hours leading up to the game were pretty uneventful; time was getting on so we headed for St. James's Park, we never saw any Wurzels, they must have been keeping their heads down, while we had the run of their city.

Once in the ground, the Exeter lads were housed to the right of us, in the aptly named Cowshed while we were housed behind the goal, 1500 of us packed in like sardines on the tiny terracing with only a small brick wall separating us from the pitch; this was easily breached by about twenty of us and an impromptu kick-about began. The police were quite good-natured and allowed us to carry on until the players took the field for their warm up.

Ten minutes into the game, amid the chants of "Sheep Shaggers! Sheep Shaggers!" and "Aberfan!" it kicked off on the Cowshed, a cry of "Cardiff!" went up and a large gap appeared on the packed terracing and we could see a handful of Neath lads getting stuck in, they were overwhelmingly outnumbered and totally surrounded by Wurzels, they took a bit of a heavy beating, luckily it was over very quickly, they got away with just a couple of blackened eyes and reddened faces. The police were straight in and dragged them out of the ground, which in those days meant you could pay again to get in; today you would be banged up and in front of a Special Court; how things have changed.

The match itself was crap, both sides couldn't score in a brothel; the atmosphere on the other hand was electric, you could feel the hatred of anything Welsh in every venomous Wurzel chant. As the match drew to a close you could feel the restlessness of the lads on both sides all itching for a row. The final whistle sounded and we headed for the exits, 250 of us, the police tried to hold us in but sheer brute force pushed them aside and we marched onwards up the hill to the main street. Exeter's lads had the same idea and as we rounded the corner there ahead of us were a mob of about 300 Wurzels. Without hesitation both mobs attacked each other; there were no police insight; it was toe to toe, the Wurzels stood firm not giving an inch I looked round for familiar faces and there on the floor was Dillys, he hurriedly scrambled to his feet before the boots came in. Exeter were on top now and they backed us across the road, sporadic scuffles broke out along the main street sending crowds of shoppers running for cover. The police arrived en masse and pushed us onto the pavement, opposite walked the Wurzels and anyone who ventured across the road got a whack from a truncheon for their trouble.

As the Wurzels shadowed our escort they passed a greengrocers with his wares on sale outside on the pavement, and suddenly we were ducking and dodging cauliflowers, cabbages and other assorted vegetables, soon a food fight broke out, we returned fire, what a farcical sight, lads from both sides being felled by turnips and cucumbers as the police looked on. The fighting continued along the long route to the train station, with Wurzels steaming out of side streets and alleys, the police were stretched and were losing control as we broke out of the escort and went one to one with the Wurzels, we finally forced them backwards the way they had came.

Reaching the station I heard a police officer say "That was the worst outbreak of football violence he had ever seen". Looking around at the lads on the platform, as we stood waiting for our train back to Cardiff, I noticed there were a number of lads who looked like they had been in a war, their once pristine stonewashed jeans were now bloodstained and covered in dirt.

Unlike their Wurzel counterparts Exeter have never ventured to Ninian Park in numbers and have never brought anything that resembled a firm, but on their own manor they can pull numbers together and I always enjoy the welcome we receive.

The Zulus

With Wembley Stadium out of commission as it undergoes a major facelift and modernisation Cardiff's Millennium Stadium was awarded the privilege of hosting all the major football finals until 2006 this was a coup for Cardiff, and all the local businesses, hotels, bars and restaurants were rubbing their hands with the thought of all the extra revenue. This would undoubtedly put Wales and the city of Cardiff in particular on the map.

One of the first showpiece finals was the 2001 Littlewoods Cup Final Liverpool versus Birmingham City to be played on a customary Sunday afternoon and the word on the street was that The Zulus would be arriving in the Capital on Saturday and staying in local Hotels and B & B's.

We hadn't heard anything about the Scousers and to be honest we weren't expecting any trouble with them; Cardiff have never had any history with Liverpool but personally I hate Scousers I think it dates back to when I used to follow Man Utd; they are all generally perceived as happy go-lucky, fun-loving, harmless cheeky chappies all with an infectious sense of humour, a firm full of Stan Boardmans and Jimmy Tarbucks but in reality I've found them all to be horrible, Stanley wielding, robbing bastards with whiney fucking accents.

The Brum on the other hand have a fair bit of history with us; the first time I visited St. Andrews was in the early eighties with Manchester United; Birmingham City were in the First Division at the time and I travelled with Dominic Ferrari a local lad who was a fanatical United supporter. United sold their allocation and as we stood on the crumbling terrace we were bombarded with coins and bricks from the Brum alongside us; the only thing separating the two sets of supporters was a mesh net, presumably set up to catch thrown missiles, even in those days St. Andrews was an intimidating place to go.

However, the first time I ventured to Small Heath with Cardiff City was in the mid to late eighties. Cardiff City were in the Second Division, alongside such teams as Chelsea, Newcastle, Sheffield Wednesday and Leeds. Birmingham City away was one of our biggest trips of the season and these types of games always brought out the big hitters and this was to be no different. The Soul Crew was out in force. There were 150 of us mobbed up on Cardiff Central Station; we had a large contingent from the Rhondda Valley, we had older lads like Trajic and Vampy, plus Mickey Villain, Lurch, Elvid, Prune and Mouldsy from Ferndale plus Cen, Ashley and myself from Porth, as well as Reesy, Mark H and the Foster brothers; also dotted around the station were lads from Port Talbot and Neath. The main faces from Cardiff were also out in force Dai H and his tight crew, the lads from the Docks plus lads from Ely and other surrounding Districts;

looking along the packed platform as we waited to board the train it was like a who's who of Football Hooligans.

By the time we reached Newport the Buffet Bar had sold out of alcohol, and we were joined by three other main players Lawson, Basil plus Alan and the lads from Cwmbran. The booze was in full flow and everyone was up for a ruck, the atmosphere was really relaxed, lads either playing cards or reading the sport pages of the weekend tabloids. The few Transport Police that were accompanying us had no problems from us and they kept a low profile.

As we neared Birmingham New Street station the usual banter was replaced by an eerie silence and as we entered the station and rose from our seats there was a look of apprehension on the faces of a few of the younger lads. We disembarked from the train, the older lads taking the lead, waiting for us were the West Midlands Old Bill who stepped in and separated us from the weekend shoppers. They led us away from the escalators to an underground walkway that would allow us to be shepherded out of the station unnoticed.

The 150 of us made our way along the narrow tunnel flanked by about two dozen Old Bill, suddenly there was a chant of "Zulus, Zulus" a few of the younger lads stopped in their tracks, while the rest of us pushed on, there was now an urgency in our step as we strode up the tunnel, it was us who were pushing the pace now not the Old Bill and we strode towards the exit. The Old Bill escorting us must have played out this scenario week in and week out but a few of them looked rather too nervous for my liking; a few of our older heads were telling everyone to stick together and keep tight.

Suddenly, out of one of the many side exits came a mob of 70 lads, this caught us and the Old Bill by surprise, scuffles broke out all around us, then the Zulus were in front of us, they were 70 handed both black and white lads together. We charged at them, steaming through the Old Bill who were now in disarray, the fighting was ferocious and one of our lads got either a hook or some kind of machete in the back of his head. The Zulus have always been known for their fondness for hardware and today was no exception. The Zulus steamed into us and it was going toe to toe at the front of the narrow tunnel, the shout of "Soul Crew, Soul Crew" went up from lads at the back and it echoed around the tunnel giving the impression of much larger numbers and we steamed in again, the police had now lost control and we pushed the Zulus out of the station and into the Bull Ring. Once out of the station there was plenty more space for a ruck and we spread out and charged the Brum again and after a couple of quick scuffles the Zulus were on the back foot; then the police reinforcements arrived and the Zulus made a hasty retreat while we were escorted from the area and towards the ground. That was game over as far as nonsense was concerned and rest of the day passed off incident free.

The last time we visited St. Andrews most of us travelled by train but Pasti, a good mate of mine made his way with a coach load of lads from The Ferndale Con Club. Our train pulled into Birmingham New Street station, 150 of us made our way up the escalators and towards the main concourse there we met a handful of lads who had made their way by car and had come unstuck just a few minutes before we arrived. We headed out of the station in the direction of The Zulus but were met by a wall of police, that was the end of our nonsense and we were escorted to the ground.

After the game there were minor scuffles breaking out in the car park with winners and losers on both sides, the police soon had us under control and we were escorted back to New Street without further ado.

Pasti and the lads from the Con on the other hand had joined the snaking convoy of coaches that made their way slowly through Brum; somehow they got separated and found themselves overlooking a children's playground.

The driver brought the coach to a stop while he found his bearings; suddenly a couple of coloured lads appeared and started bricking the coach, Pasti and the others didn't need a second invitation and soon the emergency exit was flung open and the lads were diving out into the street. They chased the lads into the playground and down a grassy bank but to their horror there on the horizon were around 50 more coloureds who came charging towards them chucking bricks and bottles; it was obviously an ambush and the twenty odd lads were vastly outnumbered and had no choice but to turn and run back to their coach. In the ensuing chase Gatesy another mate of mine who was a lot slower than the rest was hit on the back of his head with half a house brick and had to be carried onto the coach.

All the lads made it safely back onto their coach but their nightmare wasn't over yet, they soon found themselves surrounded by a mob of baying Zulus. A couple of large Frank Bruno types tried to force their way onto the coach and the lads at the front fought for their lives to prevent them getting on. The rest of the Zulus hurled everything they had at the coach and the bricks went whistling through the windows showering the lads with shards of glass, window after window were put through while Pasti, Gatesy and the others lay on the floor, helpless to stop this brutal assault. Once the bricks had run out the Zulus started to rock the coach trying to tip it over, the lads onboard were petrified and after what must have seemed like a lifetime the Old Bill finally turned up and dispersed everyone.

Back to 2001 and with Brum playing in Cardiff, this was the perfect opportunity for the Soul

Crew to turn the Zulus over. We started to mob up in The Borough on St. Mary Street just a stones throw from the Millennium Stadium, I arrived about 12:30 and joined another dozen lads, over the next couple of hours our numbers would swell to 70; our mob was mixed with valley old heads and younger Cardiff lads; on days like this its difficult to get our A Team mobbed up in town, the Old Bill just pull you in; so the majority of lads hole up in Canton normally in the Exchange and the Kings there are usually 120 lads split between the two boozers . A steady stream of Blues lads had also been arriving and our spotters had located them in The Slug and Lettuce, which was two streets behind us, only separated by a long thin street called Wharton Street.

Mid afternoon and the Blues were on the move making their way towards us, we left the Borough and turned into Wharton Street, coming towards us was a mob of about 70 lads; made up of Normals, young dressers, Shirters, seasoned lads and a sprinkling of Loons this wasn't Brum's firm but like my mate Pricey once said "You can only fight what's stood in front of you".

With numbers about equal, both firms neared each other, then like most footy rows there was the initial throwing of glasses and bottles, then the usual stand-off occurred, then we attacked each other, both firms spread out across the narrow street, it was toe to toe, punches and boots flying in, we had the upper hand and pushed the Zulus back; then a couple of van loads of Old Bill were on the scene sending lads from both firms flying, as we all tried to evade arrest. I made my way back to The Borough, most of us had the same idea and soon there were fifty of us plotting our next attack.

Within fifteen minutes the boozer was swarming with police, who instructed the landlord to close for the day; and we were unceremoniously turfed out onto St. Mary Street, which was awash with CCTV Cameras and by now was cordoned off with police vans blocking every side street.

Later in the day it was reported Brum were mobbed up in the RSVP Bar; formerly the Owain Glyndwr, in St. Johns Square; we walked up the small lane to confront them, we had about 50 lads present and as soon as we were spotted the doors flew open and the Brum flew out at us; this was their firm a mix of both blacks and whites and plenty of old heads. We squared up to each other us older heads taking the lead, scuffles broke out all over the thin alleyway, one on ones broke out as it went toe to toe; after about 30 seconds the Brum were on top they came through our front line and we disintegrated, lads were tripping over each other to get away the Brum were now in full flight and chased us onto St. Mary Street. The Old Bill were soon on hand to restore order and rounded us lot up while they escorted the Zulus out of the area.

Our every move was now being monitored and the Old Bill were constantly pushing us further out of the city centre. The Brum lads had also been moved on; to the bottom of St. Mary Street and the Mill Lane area of the city, the bulk of their mob were now drinking in The Walkabout Our numbers had been cut to around twenty five as the police went about splitting us up.

As luck had it we came across a small mob of Brum in Dempsey's, an Irish bar opposite the castle; we tried to get through the doors but with the help of the bouncers the Zulus kept us out. Some of the lads ran into the adjoining lane and came back with scaffolding poles, stools and chairs and tried to batter down the small front doors, the doors stood firm, so the windows were put through as the Brum cowered inside; soon the wailing of sirens meant it was time for us to fuck off into the night.

Unlike the Zulus we were finding it increasingly difficult to get a drink, most boozers were refusing to let groups of blokes in, so we split into groups of threes and fours and I found myself with some younger Cardiff lads. We headed back towards St. Mary Street to try our luck; blending in with the weekend revellers; this is where the bulk of the boozers are located.

There were five of us trying to keep a low profile; while the police were very visible, carrying out stop and searches on anyone who looked remotely football. We decided to try the City Arms, this was a small boozer nestled in a narrow side street; coming towards us were a handful of leather clad lads, we walked towards each other, they spotted us and a few of them put their heads down trying to avoid eye contact, as we drew level one of the Cardiff lads gave one of them a punch in the mush, a couple of them were immediately on their toes, heads down arses up but two of them stood; one was a short fat coloured lad, the other was a white bloke, a man mountain in a three quarter leather coat. I set about the shorter lad, we swapped a couple of blows then one of our lot caught him with a boot and a couple of blows to the head and he too was on his toes; the larger bloke though was having none of it, and was keeping three Cardiff lads at bay with some big hits, he was bringing the fight to us, he came passed me so I decided to give him a wide berth, still throwing punches he made his way safely out of the narrow street; I don't think a single punch landed on him.

The Bouncers at The City Arms wouldn't let us in, so we made our way to the Rummer Tavern in Castle Street, success at last and we settled down for a couple of pints, there were small groups of us in pubs all over the city centre, the mobile phones were red hot as everyone tried to regroup but it was futile, the Old Bill, Bouncers and the Landlords had the night sewn up.

At chucking out time little mobs of The Soul Crew started to get together and made their way to the bottom of St. Mary Street; that is where the majority of the Zulus were drinking. The Brum tried to make a move up St. Mary Street around 11 O'clock and the two rival mobs clashed outside the Philharmonic which was consequently trashed; its large bay windows being put through and the violence was so bad that two of the neighbouring pubs were forced to close. The

Old Bill battled to restore order but the ferocious fighting raged on; the violence led to nine lads being hospitalised one seriously injured. The Old Bill finally got on top and pushed the Zulus back towards the Walkabout. With the large number of Brum followers in the city; it was safe to say there were pockets of Brum lads drinking all over the city centre and sporadic outbreaks of violence raged on until the early hours of the morning with winners and losers on both sides. That was the last time we mixed it with the Zulus of Birmingham F.C. and there were winners and losers on both sides but our paths will cross soon enough with Birmingham having been relegated from the Premiership last season. I have a lot of respect for The Zulus they can mix it with the best of them and I'm sure there are lads from both firms looking forward to doing battle next season.

Oldham Athletic Away

It was the beginning of another season, Oldham Athletic was our first away fixture of 2002 and we're going by train for a change, over the last couple of years we've mainly been travelling by private coaches or Battle Buses.

Pasti, Jimmy, Dion and myself left Pontypridd station nice and early, we were soon joined by Peter at Taffs Well and we're heading for Cardiff Central, I hadn't travelled by train for so long I didn't know what to expect, I was well aware that only a small number of lads regularly use the train so I wasn't expecting too many Soul Crew to greet us. Milling around in the concourse of Cardiff Central were our mates Woodsy, Pricey and Christian also dotted around was Kirby from Ebbw Vale plus two young lads I had never met.

Eleven of us, we made our way onto the platform and waited for the train, the train duly arrived, Gary from Neath was already aboard and was in the company of five lads, none of whom looked like rowing material, we gave Gary a nod and took our seats in a separate carriage. Gary was a good lad, I had seen him in action on a number of occasions, he would never let you down, but only twelve lads this was a real poor show, not that we were worried about Oldham, they were so lame they needed Stockport and Shrewsbury to back them up.

Class A's and the drinks trolley helped us wile away the hours, we pulled into Shrewsbury and there were a handful of lads of the English Border Firm stood on the platform, a couple of our lads went to the doors but the Shrewsbury declined our offer to join us. We pulled into Manchester Piccadilly and made our way to Wetherspoons, the boozer was quite full with local lunchtime drinkers, we made our way to the bar and we spotted Alan from Cwmbran, Scot from Carlisle and a handful of North Walian lads from Holyhead and Llandudno Junction, there were also a small group of Man Utd lads stood around the fruit machines; they were on their way to watch United against Boca Juniors of Argentina. Alan was a Legend amongst the Soul Crew and had been on the scene since the beginning; he had recognised one of the United lads from a past scuffle in Cardiff; their paths had crossed when United had visited the Millennium Stadium. Alan made his way over to him; the Manc was a big lad, both tall and chunky, Alan asked him if the Mancs had a firm out, the lad shrugged his shoulders and the Manc contingent soon left the pub. We had to get to Manchester Victoria station for our connection to Oldham, our numbers now totalled eighteen still pretty poor, we made the long walk across the city. We arrived at Victoria, we had about fifteen minutes to wait for our train and as we hung around at the station entrance we soon noticed a small group of lads coming down the hill towards us amongst them was the

- 73 -

Manc from earlier. Here we go I thought; we outnumbered the Mancs three to one but still they kept coming, personally I thought this was a set up, enticing us to chase them up the hill where no doubt there would be a larger number of them waiting. We decided to stand firm and see how far they would venture down the hill, we spread out across the road in full view of the oncoming Mancs and still they came and as they neared us Jimmy, Pasti and a couple of others charged towards them, this is what the Mancs had wanted and they turned and fled back up the hill but our lads gave up the chase and returned to the station; we were sure that this wouldn't be the end of it and that we would see more of the Mancs later on.

We boarded the train and arrived in Oldham, the eighteen of us made our way to Boundary Park, as we neared the ground we came across a boozer situated on the main road, just a short distance from the ground, We called in for a pint; and the vast majority decided they were going on the piss, so just Dion and myself went to the match, this was a new stadium for me so I was determined to do the ground. I hadn't done many new grounds lately; you know how it is, you seem to go to the same grounds year after year, places where there will be an off, and to teams you have a history with.

Sat in the stands at Boundary Park Oldham, observing another inept City performance, the roar of "Blooobirds, Blooobirds", from the three thousand City faithful packed behind the goal suddenly transported me back to my first ever away match…it was the beginning of the 1981 season and City had drawn Torquay United in the first round of the League Cup at Plainmoor.

Andrew Watkins and I had decided to make the four-hour journey to follow our beloved City. We had started supporting the City the earlier season and had attended a few home games but up until now we had never ventured away.

It was a bright sunny Saturday morning in August, I hadn't slept much, the excitement and adrenalin racing through my veins had made it almost impossible, I lay most of the night staring at the clock. Dressed in the fashion of the day, tight T shirts, light summer jackets, flared denim jeans, Dr Martin boots and the must have, blue and white Cardiff City scarf tied tightly around the right wrist, no Burberry, Stone Island or other expensive designer labels like the fashion conscious terrace dweller of today.

We arrived at the cenotaph; there were already a group of men assembled. The coach arrived at 8 O'clock sharp and we clambered aboard, finding a window seat Andrew and I settled down for the journey ahead. The coach was organised by Roy and Mair Daniels a married couple who ran Adar Glas (Blue Birds) Supporters Club. Those days were so much more innocent, no alcohol allowed just pop and crisps, a far cry from the organised mayhem of the Battle Buses that I would travel on in later years. The coach was good-natured, with a family atmosphere and there was an air of optimism aboard.

We finally arrived at Plainmoor; outside the ground were hundreds of City fans milling around and the atmosphere was really friendly. We entered the ground and made our way onto the small terracing behind the goal, the aroma of hotdogs and burgers filled the air. The kick off drew closer and the City fans started to swell the tiny terracing, the atmosphere was rising, we were both filled with anticipation, and were enjoying the banter from both sets of supporters. Torquay were housed in the home end directly opposite us at the far end of the ground. The players took their place on the field. Our heroes received a rousing chorus of "Blooobirds! Blooobirds!" the game kicked off, the speed was breakneck with crunching tackles a plenty, but no team could take control, we tried to spur our players on with chants of encouragement "C'mon City, c'mon City", and "Get in to 'em, get in to 'em", our throats grew hoarse but you couldn't beat that feeling. The ninety minutes meant everything in those days, looking back I can see how cynical I've become, and how I now attend matches looking for something completely different, and needless to say, now I travel in the company of the Firm, not good old Roy and Mair. The referee blew for half time; we both checked our watches time had seemed to have flown. The game was no masterpiece but we didn't care as the atmosphere and camaraderie made up for the lack of skill on display. We joined the snaking queue for a hotdog during the interval, both of us chattering incessantly. We made our way back onto the cramped terracing, struggling through the throng to find a good vantage point for the second half, we got settled and the game kicked off. We were both hoping that the second half would improve and that we could get the all-decisive goal.

Once again the pace was hectic, no quarter being asked and none given but once again neither team could make the breakthrough, and it's a case of a bad final pass and possession all too easily squandered. The atmosphere was still great though and we were pushed forward and back as our team attacked, the noise reached fever pitch whenever we entered the opposition goalmouth, or whenever we succeeded in forcing a corner, but the elusive goal just wouldn't come and the closest anyone came to scoring was when Torquay hit the crossbar. At that moment our hearts were in our mouths and you could hear the whole end sigh with relief as the ball rebounded harmlessly out of play. The final whistle blew and it was a disappointing 0-0 no score bore draw, and as the two teams trundled off down the tunnel the City fans hurdled the small brick wall at the front of the terracing and across the pitch towards the set of home supporters. Football matches weren't heavily policed like nowadays. Firstly a small trickle clambered over the wall, then a torrent and somehow Andrew and I were caught up in the excitement and found ourselves hurtling headlong down the terracing and we both vaulted the wall, once on the pitch we stared at each other not knowing what to do next, then totally out of character I took the lead and charged with the rest across the field leaving Andrew in my wake. I was a lot fitter in those days and I soon neared the halfway line, with my heart in my mouth. Further in front of me, some City fans tried to negotiate the large fence that penned the home supporters in. The Torquay fans stampeded as they tried to escape the clutches of the baying Taffy hoardes, this was the first taking of an "end" I had witnessed, the small number of police on duty battled bravely to restore order and with the use of police dogs managed to disperse the City faithful. I stood on the halfway line and saw hundreds of bodies hurtling in my direction. In a fit of panic I turned and ran towards the safety of the away terracing from whence I came, faster and faster I ran, my heart racing, I didn't dare look 'round and didn't stop until I had safely made it back over the small brick wall. What a rush I thought, I trembled from head to toe, I bristled, full of so many different emotions and although I never saw any violence I was hooked. We all left the ground to chants of "Lenny Ashurst's blue and white army!" I caught up with Andrew in a street outside the ground, some City fans were still in pursuit of home supporters, but we weren't up for that, we both made our way to the coach park, we'd seen enough excitement for one day, we were still bouncing. On our long journey home, all we spoke about was the pitch invasion, strangely the game itself wasn't even mentioned.

"Blooobirds! Blooobirds!" suddenly I'm dragged back to the present day. City have scored and the City faithful are delirious. I look around me at the designer clad firm, and think of how sterile all-seater stadia has made the game I love, I managed a wry smile to myself and joined in the chant "Blooobirds! Blooobirds!"

The game disintegrated into a type of long-ball tennis with both teams hoofing the ball back and fro; my mind wasn't on the football but on what might have been happening outside and of what I might have been missing. I had to rejoin the lads; I'd done the ground so I left and headed straight for the boozer.

I made my way along the main road, but the lads had left, I could see them in the distance heading for another nearby pub. I caught up with them as they arrived at the pub's entrance; in the windows were a number of Oldham's lads, who like us had decided to give the game a miss. We made our way to the large wooden doors, they were locked; more Oldham came to the windows, some with pool cues in their hands, they were taunting us and calling us on, a couple of our lot started to kick at the doors while others were banging on the windows, we were making our intentions known in no uncertain terms but the Oldham refused to come and join us for a bit of sport. The kicking of the doors continued but we couldn't break them down and soon a van load of Old Bill arrived on the scene and escorted us back to the earlier pub, where they stayed and monitored our every move. I've never rated Oldham and this re-enforced my belief that they were a just a small team with a gutless, ragtag mob.

With around five minutes remaining of the match we left the pub and headed back to Boundary Park, we mobbed-up in the large car park and waited for the final whistle; an awful lot of violent clashes take place in and around the car parks of football grounds up and down the country; week in and week out. The fans started streaming out into the car park, we looked on as hundreds of shirts and scarfers passed us and made their way to their cars; pretty soon Dion joined us but Oldham's lads were nowhere to be seen, we made our way around to the Home End looking for a bit of nonsense but it wasn't to be.

We left the ground and headed for the train station; we had now been joined by Clayton a muscular coloured lad from Cardiff who was an Ex-Professional boxer. Our route took us through a large Asian community; where we were met with the strong aroma of curries and unwelcoming looks from the locals; they must have thought a mob of predominantly white blokes walking through their neighbourhood must have been looking for trouble; but this couldn't have been further from the truth; for it's a fact that only a tiny minority of Cardiff's firm have extremist right-wing beliefs; and in the twenty odd years I've been in the firm we have never had a major problem with racism.

We boarded the train to Victoria and the Mancs from earlier were on all our minds, would there be a welcoming committee awaiting our arrival in the city centre. We made our way over the footbridge and out of the station; nothing, no one, no Old Bill and more importantly no Mancs. We headed towards Piccadilly and the city centre, the plan was to have a couple of pints before catching our train home. After walking for about ten minutes in the middle of the Arndale Centre we came to a Continental type of bar, with a large outdoor seating area, situated in a kind of basin with large white steps surrounding it. It was a very busy bar full of early evening drinkers and young couples taking advantage of the pleasant Summer weather.

The lads took their drinks and congregated at the top of the steps; Pasti, Jimmy and myself were the last to get served and were still in the bar when we noticed Dion waving frantically at us. We left our beers and rushed outside. The Mancs had turned up and after a quick scuffle had backed our lads down the first couple of steps. We bounded up the steps to join the lads; the first thing we noticed was Scott's eye, he had a large gash across his eyebrow where he had been glassed and was bleeding profusely.

The Northerners were looking down on us; they had the upper hand, it was their usual faces, a large Asian lad was fronting them, they had a big coloured lad, the lad from Wetherspoons and a short stocky ginger lad with them; these were the same lads we had rowed with in Cardiff.

Insults and threats were traded; Alan was giving them plenty of verbal; there were equal numbers on each side and I had my eye on a stocky lad in a black leather jacket. The Asian bloke seemed their top lad, he was giving it the big un, he lunged down the steps at us and Pricey hit him with an uppercut that sent him sprawling backwards and left him pole-axed on the ground; that was our cue, we all bounced up the steps and straight into them, the big coloured lad took a couple of big hits to the head and he too was lying on the floor, we were all in amongst them, boots and fist flying furiously. The tables had turned; the Northerners were on the back foot now and our Ex boxer had one of their lads cornered against a back wall and was hitting him with both jabs and combinations I had never seen such fast hands at work, the beleaguered Manc had no reply, Christian was setting about the ginger lad and Alan was giving another hapless lad a good hiding. We were well on top and none of us took a backwards step from then on and we pushed the Mancs back towards the shopping centre; as the fighting raged on our attention was brought to the Asian lad who was in trouble and we thought he had swallowed his tongue. The fighting had now stopped, the welfare of the Asian lad now took priority. There were lads sprawled all over the floor, and as they got to their feet, two of the defeated Mancs sheepishly came over and picked him up and carried him off and then everybody shook hands and we all went our own separate ways.

We were bouncing, a few chants of "Soul Crew, Soul Crew" and we headed towards Piccadilly station; there's no better feeling than turning over a rival firm especially when its one of the so called top firms in the country.

The six rows I've described above were the best I've personally been involved in; and the same small band of blokes were by my side in most of them, lads I would gladly trust with my life and lads I would do anything for. I've known these blokes since 1982, when we were all naïve teenagers in love with the fashions and the thrill of football violence. We have been on the scene ever since, through the good and bad times plus the Rave and Ecstasy fuelled periods and are now elder statesmen of the Soul Crew. These lads wouldn't let you down, but I'm not so stupid to suggest that these lads have never run, because all firms get run, and anyone who disagrees is a liar.

CHAPTER SEVEN

EVERY DAY I WAKE UP I THANK GOD I'M WELSH

Being Welsh sets us apart from all the other British nations, for we have our own unique culture and a language which is over two thousand years old, which at this moment is on the increase throughout Wales.

But being Welsh means different things to different people, personally being Welsh is to have a proud sense of our traditions and our culture and the Welsh valleys are full of males with the uncanny ability to consume endless supplies of lukewarm beer while fighting and standing up singing; being Welsh is having a ready sense of humour that is often self mocking and having a passionate sense of local identity; being Welsh to me begins with my Mam and Dad and is a heady cocktail of history and family, blood and pride. Being Welsh is also afternoons spent in smoke-filled bookies and watching football played in misty grounds on Boxing Day; being Welsh is seeing the faults of my nation but loving it just the same and knowing that although my country is forever changing that some things remain eternal like our ferocious belief in fairness and we're willing to fight to defend it, we love the plucky underdog and we have a tremendous in-built ability to laugh at ourselves, this is a very Welsh thing. Being Welsh is retaining our enduring faith in our sporting teams and heroes and a shared pride in their achievements.

In the mainly English speaking South the importance of our language and our future Independence from England plus our own Welsh Assembly is less than in the Bi-lingual North and Mid Wales. Wales is very diverse for such a small nation with only a population of around three million, and there is no true Welsh Accent. There are the Welsh speaking heartlands of North Wales that sound nothing like the South Wales valleys, the North Walian Scousers, the mockneys of Cardiff, the Wurzels of Newport and Monmouthshire plus the softly spoken accent of the Swansea valleys all these different accents take their place alongside each other within the rich tapestry of Wales and Welshness.

We are a Celtic nation and have been settled on the British Isles longer than any other group of people; from Cumbria in the North of England, the Midlands, and the West Country were once all Welsh lands, the first Welsh Kings held court in Cumbria, this was our Capital and this is where the word Cymru meaning Wales is derived.

Over the years our land was stolen from us by the Angles and Saxons who are the modern day English, and our way of life, culture and language has been slowly eroded. Many tribes invaded Britain including the Romans who conquered everything before them, but the Welsh have never been conquered by anyone, to demonstrate this there are more castles and forts and other defences in Wales than anywhere else in the World. We are a fighting nation, plus we have a strong passion for poetry and song, and although we are a very diverse nation two things unite the Welsh people; firstly our flag Y Ddraig Goch which is The Red Dragon and secondly the hatred of anything English.

Being a supporter of Cardiff City and being a passionate Welshman it was an easy transition to make to support the National team and over the years these two passions went hand in hand. The first Welsh matches I watched were the Home International Championships I watched Wales play Scotland at the Vetch in Swansea, Northern Ireland at Ninian Park Cardiff and England both at Ninian Park and Wembley but my first trip abroad was to Czechoslovakia.

These are the most memorable Welsh matches both Home and Away I've attended.

Czechoslovakia 1981

The World Cup Qualifiers of 1982 found us in the same group as:- Iceland, Russia, Turkey and Czechoslovakia; and after a good start to our campaign the match against Czechoslovakia was the most appealing away trip. I was just seventeen when Wales played Czechoslovakia in Prague, it was the 9th September 1981; Andrew Watkins and I were determined to follow our national heroes; we had both just left school and had gained placements on a Youth Training Scheme; we both worked for the same company; I was in the Payroll Department while Andrew worked in the workshop, so as you can imagine cash was tight. Luckily my mother and father both clubbed together, at the time my mother was saving 50 pence pieces in a large glass jar supposedly for a rainy day, it totalled £50 which she gave me; while my father always had two cars on the go, one being a beige Hillman Hunter which I was able to sell for £200, plus over the weeks I managed to save £50 from my pay; armed with £300 I was sorted. Andrew tried to save as much of his pay as possible because being one of four kids he didn't want to rely solely on his parents for cash.

With Czechoslovakia being situated in Eastern Europe and within the so-called "Iron Curtain" both Passports and Visas were compulsory to enter the country. This was to be my first trip abroad; my family couldn't afford Summer holidays to the likes of Spain, we made do with a fortnight in a caravan in Porthcawl, a small seaside town in South Wales.

The trip was booked and we travelled by coach with Roy and Mair Daniels and Adar Glas. The coach was made up of mainly middle-aged blokes but situated towards the rear of the coach were a dozen or so lads in their early twenties including: Bruno, Mario, Gorkey, Woodsy, Bishop and Fat Dai these were the hooligans of the time, these lads were veterans of travelling away with Wales and Cardiff City.

We left the Rhondda valley and headed for the port of Folkestone where we would pick up a ferry to the Hook of Holland. We were booked on a night sailing; once onboard we met another coach load of blokes from Cardiff; we all made our way to one of the many bars onboard and settled down for the long crossing. On the upper deck was a cheesy Disco playing tunes like The Birdie Song, Oops Upside Your Head and Hi Ho Silver Lining by Jeff Beck; although it was really naff it seemed to keep the lads amused.

This was my first encounter with alcohol and I threw myself right into the swing of things, drank far too much and made a right tit of myself and spent most of the crossing in the bog throwing up. We arrived at the Hook of Holland around 6.00a.m. I felt like shit, my head and guts felt like I'd been hit by a train, I gingerly boarded the coach, there were some right hung over blokes and the coach stank of stale booze, fags and farts. We headed for the German city of Cologne where we would be spending the night, hours later and what seemed like an eternity we finally arrived at our destination; it was around 7.00p.m.

We checked into our hotel and hit the pubs with the older lads, there were about fifteen of us, safety in numbers made sense and after a couple of pints we headed for the Red Light District; this was an eye-opener for Andrew and I, we stared at the scantily clad beauties and even for the older lads this was still something of a novelty. Soon the lads made their way down a flight of steps and we sheepishly followed and we were soon inside an upmarket brothel or Gentlemen's Club as the German's preferred. Andrew and I were well out of our depth and just followed the older lads, we got a beer at the bar and stared open mouthed at the topless young girls on display. The club was decked out with rich burgundy soft furnishings and plush carpets nothing like I imagined it would be, I thought it would be tacky, plastic looking and overall tasteless.

The girls would make their way over to us and we were all encouraged to buy them a drink, but at £25 a time, it was a bit rich for us, and this pissed a couple of the lads off and there was a simmering undercurrent which didn't go unnoticed by the club's door staff. I could sense something nasty was going to happen, so Andrew and I slipped away from the bar and pretty soon there was an argument in the bar area, initially raised voices then a bit of pushing and shoving then one of our lads stuck the head in and it all kicked off, punches were thrown by both sides, the Germans were big blokes and could clearly handle themselves, they gave as good as they got and stood their ground. With a couple of mighty punches they had one of our lads on the floor and pushed the rest of the boys towards the exit, the Germans were no mugs and took total control of the situation and a couple of swift punches later and the lads were out on the street. There were only a handful of us left and looking at the door staff I thought we were going to get filled in, I was shitting myself to be honest; my stomach was so knotted I couldn't drink my beer.

Andrew and I just sat motionless on the sofa wishing we were invisible; but luckily we had nothing to worry about; a young brunette girl came over to me, she was gorgeous; but being only seventeen I had very little sexual experience, once again I was shitting myself; but once again I needn't have worried because she took good care of me if you know what I mean.

The following morning we checked out and congregated outside our hotel, while we waited to board the coach to Prague. A couple of lads turned up with bruised and swollen faces and fat Dai was taking the piss out of one of his mates who had whip marks all over his back, he was in a lot of pain, but had obviously had his money worth.

We arrived in Prague two days before the match, we dropped our bags off at the Jalta Hotel and explored the City. Czechoslovakia was under Russian control at this time and the Hammer and Sickle was etched into every lamp post to serve as a reminder to the Czech people. Prague at this time was run by the state police and talking to Westerners was severely frowned upon, as we walked around the city there was the feel of Big Brother about the place and large black limousines were never too far away from us, as if watching our every move.

The armed Czech police saw us as easy prey and on the spot fines were meted out for everything from crossing the street to simply talking; this money was pocketed by the police themselves, this seemed to be one of the many perks of the job.

We spent our first night in Prague in a large bar in the Jewish Quarter of the city; there must have been about 250 of us Welsh fans there, and what shocked me was that many were Ex-Pats living in England; there were a large contingent from London and the South East, lads from Bolton, Preston, Wigan and Blackpool plus lads from the Midlands and the West Country there were even Geordies and a bloke that lived in Scotland. Some supported English league teams although the majority supported Cardiff City but they were all united behind the Welsh cause.

The following day the team were arriving, so we all planned to go to the airport to greet them, around 300 of us made the short journey by train to the airport. We had a couple of hours to wait for their flight so we all headed for the bar. The beer was flowing and we were all in good voice but the police weren't overly happy about our presence or our large numbers and once again spot fines were dished out to all and sundry, mainly for singing, although other minor misdemeanours were punished too. This pissed us all off and you could feel the animosity rising and there was a lot of anger vented at the over zealous police.

The flight finally arrived and we made our way to greet our heroes and as they came down the steps onto the runway we all ran to the windows; chants of "Wales! Wales!" rang out around the airport bar. The police lost the plot at this point and started to push us away from the windows and shoved us towards the arrivals lounge but the blokes at the front were having none of it and scuffles broke out and around a dozen lads burst through the police lines and made their way out onto the roof. The police tried to cordon the area off and were using their batons indiscriminately, they forced the rest of us out of the bar, we all regrouped and fought back against them, I had visions of the police opening fire on us but this didn't stop the bulk of lads at the front as they fought on, kicking and punching and finally they too broke through the cordon and onto the roof and joined the other lads. The police now realised they were fighting a losing battle and had a rethink and finally let us all out onto the roof where the police kept a close eye on us and the rest of our stay at the airport was monitored very closely.

As well as the players there were around 200 Wrexham supporters on the flight, we chanted, and waved our flags and the players waved and showed their appreciation of our support; this is all we wanted to do; we never went to the airport intent on trouble but just for the chance of a glimpse of our heroes; who we all spent thousands of pounds a year on, but it was all marred by ignorant over zealous policing and it was more luck than judgement that no one was seriously hurt.

On the evening of the game, we left the hotel and caught a tram to the stadium, there were about fifty of us. We found a small bar around the stadium where we rubbed shoulders with Czech fans; we were well outnumbered but the atmosphere was friendly with both sets of fans mingling freely but all this was about to change. We left the bar and headed for the Away section, there were fifty of us, mainly middle aged blokes plus Fat Dai and his mates, we got onto the stadium's concourse when a group of about one hundred Czechs came at us all dressed in workers overalls and dungarees shouting and screaming, we backed off immediately but they came straight at us, they steamed straight in; a flying kick knocked a bloke standing by me right of his feet. I wanted to run but didn't know where; Dai and his mates stood their ground and took the brunt of the attack while we managed to run to the safety of the stadium's entrance and took our place in the ground. I heard later that Dai and the lads had come off second best but Dai had put a few Czechs on their arses.

Once inside the ground we were left alone, our numbers now totalled 600 and we felt a lot safer, we sat back and watched Wales lose 2-0; Dai Davies our keeper lived up to his nicknames of "Dai the Drop" and "Dai Teflon" by letting in goals from all of 40 yards and that was the death of another World Cup campaign.

After the match the majority of us went to a city nightclub to drown our sorrows, the club was packed but there were no Czechs, they were under curfew and had to be off the streets by 11pm. The club was full of Poles, Russians, Hungarians and other Eastern Europeans, plus obnoxious Germans; who once they found out we were Welsh started to take the piss about the score and pretty soon one of the mouthy Krauts was sent sprawling over a table, sending glasses smashing everywhere a few other Krauts steamed in and a full scale brawl erupted; the music stopped and the lights came on and the doormen tried to restore order, but on and on went the melee, chairs, stools and tables were being used as weapons and blokes of both sides were beaten to the floor. Finally the police arrived and started whacking everyone in their path; we were forced outside and pinned up against a wall; I thought we were going to get nicked but all they wanted was our cash; they rifled through our pockets, took what they wanted and fucked off into the night. We returned to our hotel knackered but relieved and personally I had had enough of Czech hospitality and couldn't wait to fuck off home.

The Dutch

As part of the 1990 World Cup Qualifiers we were drawn in the same group as Holland, Finland and West Germany, a very tough group and none of us held out any hope of us qualifying but there were some good away trips. The Away match was on 14th of September 1988 in Amsterdam and The Soul Crew were going in numbers; the relaxed Drug laws, the famous Red Light District plus the Firms of Ajax and Feyernoord, all these features appealed to us.

We mobbed up in the Philharmonic pub in St. Mary Street on the Sunday lunchtime there were about 150 Soul Crew assembled including; Keith, Reesy, Foster, Hicksy and I this was the first time the Soul Crew had followed Wales en masse and looking around the bar there was a sea of Head bags and Leathers.

We caught the train to Paddington and on the journey I had foolishly joined the lads in a game of Three Card Brag and had been liberated of £50; cash I could hardly afford to lose. We took the Tube to Liverpool Street and then the Boat Train to Harwich.

We were booked onto a night sailing; waiting for us as we boarded were a group of Transport Police who were making the crossing with us; we were forced to surrender our Passports and were to redeem them in Holland this was done to ensure a trouble free journey. We all headed for the disco, as well as the 150 of us there were about 100 Wrexham the majority being families and straight heads but as the beer flowed freely down our throats a couple of lippy Gogs came over to us and the mood rapidly changed. Moody and I were eyeball to eyeball with these blokes; Moody whacked the one and I whacked the other a bit of a scuffle ensued and a couple of lads dived in and broke it up; one of the Gogs was left bloodied and bruised and the Police were soon on the scene, Moody was nicked while I legged it to another part of the ship.

Being bladdered it wasn't long before I picked a fight with someone else; one of the ship's Pursers this time. He was having a go because I was drunk and to be honest I lost the plot, not being able to communicate properly with him, in my frustration I stuck the head on him and immediately heard the "crack" of his nose. I was suddenly jumped on by a couple of passengers and held until the police arrived; I thought "I'm in trouble now".

I was placed in the ship's cells to sober up and in the morning I faced my victim; full of remorse I was given three options:- being deported, being charged with assault and attending court in Amsterdam this could also include being put on remand until the court case or pay my victim compensation for his injuries; the latter seemed the best possible option and after some haggling we agreed on £100; I was running out of cash fast. Moody on the other hand chose deportation for his part in the row with the Gogs and he never set foot in Holland.

By the time I was released from custody the ship was deserted and the lads had left for Amsterdam. I arrived in Amsterdam in the evening and got a cabin on one of the boats berthed behind the train station. I caught up with Keith and the lads drinking in the Flying Dutchman just across the road from the station. Inside were the lads from the Soul Crew, plus a dozen Bangor City lads; we hit it off with the Bangor lads immediately and while in Amsterdam The Three Musketeers and The Flying Dutchman were our main pubs, mainly because of their prime location and their close proximity to the train station. More and more lads were turning up throughout the night including lads from Newport and lads from the Wrexham Frontline. Later that night, a handful of Caernarfon lads or Cofis as we call them arrived and the mood immediately changed; there were obviously old scores to be settled between Bangor and the Cofis and pretty soon Harvey from Bangor was straight into a coloured lad; in the ensuing scuffle glasses were smashed and tables overturned and in the mayhem the black lad was stabbed and the Bangor lads disappeared into the darkness.

The following night I met up with Keith and the lads and after a couple of liveners we headed for the Red Light District, we slowly scanned all the windows, the girls were stunning; and Hicksy was having his fill trying to service as many as physically possible. Once Hicksy had satisfied his hunger, we went looking for a different boozer and on the way we all stopped for a piss; there were cars parked both sides of the street with trees in the middle of the street so we were pissing against the trees when this guy turned up. I personally didn't take much notice but I could see he was waving something about in his hand but none of us were expecting it to be a pistol; he pointed it at us and was ranting and raving in Dutch, he certainly didn't seem happy and the lads didn't need to be told twice and dived for cover; while Hicksy went Zig Zagging down the street others took refuge behind cars leaving me standing there. He turned the shooter on me, I just stared at him with my cock hanging out, he walked over to me and pointed the gun at my head, I thought "here we go", "Fuck Off!" he shouted and pointed down the street; I zipped up my flies and walked off, as I walked I was waiting for a shot to ring out but thankfully it never came. Once I was out of sight and more importantly out of range I set out to look for the lads; I dived into the nearest bar; there was no sign of the lads but luckily there were a group of Welsh lads there. I told them of my encounter with the mad gunman, they listened but didn't take me too seriously, and one of the group a tall, ginger, Newport Skinhead more or less called me a liar, so I took him outside, followed by the rest of the lads and headed up the street to where the gunman was earlier. As we neared the spot the nutter jumped out from behind a parked car and grabbed the Skinhead gentleman and placed the gun against his head. I thought to myself I've been here before and i've never seen the colour drain from someone so quick the lad went grey and his legs went limp as he pleaded for his life but luckily the bloke released him and told us to fuck off. I couldn't help laughing to myself as I went in search of Keith and the lads.

The afternoon of the match was spent drinking in The Flying Dutchman, there were about 300 of us everybody had seemed to mob up there. The police turned up with about six vans, they planned to escort us to the ground but we weren't having that, so along with the Bangor lads we slipped away; there were twenty of us and we had managed to get close to the ground without being detected by the Dutch Old Bill. Close to the ground we passed a large Café Bar full of Dutch, they were sitting both inside and out, this didn't bother us because the atmosphere between us and the Dutch had been quite friendly, so we weren't expecting any trouble. We passed the bar and a Dutch chant went up and a chair was thrown at us hitting one of the Bangor lads; we charged at them, the guys sitting outside took the full brunt of our attack and were sent fleeing into the bar, the tables and chairs were hurled through the glass windows and doors as the Dutch cowered inside. The police came from everywhere and we were soon on our toes but their batons were more like whips with an almighty reach and I took a couple of lashes to the back of my head that almost knocked me off my feet but luckily I managed to stagger away and we fled onto one of the many city trams and made our way to the stadium.

Inside the stadium was about 800 of us, including a firm of about 300 made up of mainly Soul Crew, Wrexham Frontline, Bangor Warfare, Newport and smaller North Walian firms. During the game was the usual anti-Swansea shit but the majority of the violence was confined to the Dutch End, as Ajax and Feyenoord went toe to toe. On the pitch we lost 1-0 to a Ruud Gullit header in the latter stages of the match.

At the final whistle we steamed out of the stadium and towards a mob of Dutch lads, we charged straight in, the lads that stood were given a slap but most of their lads scattered into the darkness. We headed back to The Flying Dutchman, we drowned our sorrows for a couple of hours and when our numbers had diminished a number of Dutch lads dressed in large leather jackets came for a mooch but they were soon sent on their way by lads of the Frontline who chased them up a side street and into the night, for the next couple of hours we were on high alert as we awaited their return, they knew where we were and we were sure that it would be only a matter of time before their firm would show but they never did and we drifted off in separate directions.

On the whole the Dutch were very disappointing; considering they had clubs like Ajax, Feyernoord and Den Haag all of whom had an hooligan following; we were able to take the piss and we were free do any thing we liked.

The Dutch were also a disappointment in Cardiff in the return leg; their supporters were mainly families done up in orange shirts with Ruud Gullit wigs plus the nauseating brass band that follows their national team.

The Germans

Cologne was to be our next trip it was November 1989; the Soul Crew were well up for a crack at the Germans, there's always a fierce rivalry between the British and the Krauts, mainly because of the two World Wars they started; plus outside of Britain at that time they were one of the few countries that had an hooligan following and after taking the piss with the Dutch we looked forward to getting it on with the Germans.

We met at Cardiff Central train Station; the plan was to head for Amsterdam to taste more of the Dutch Delights; then hit Cologne on the day of the game. Our numbers were down on the Dutch trip, there were about 60 Soul Crew including Foster, Reesy, Keith and I of the Inter Valley Firm (IVF) plus Guff and the lads of the Port Talbot Pure Violence Mob (PVM); although we all came under the Soul Crew umbrella, the IVF and PVM were two tasty firms within the much larger firm, this often lead to animosity between the lads of the rival factions.

We negotiated the crossing to Holland with very little incident and arrived in Amsterdam for a couple days of drunken debauchery. With plenty of booze and Class A's to keep us amused our time spent in Amsterdam was just a blur to me, with very little sleep.

On the day of the game we met up with Kevin, Josh and the lads from Bangor and boarded the train to Cologne.

Once aboard the train Guff unfurled his 40ft Union Jack flag, and about 30 minutes into our journey proceeded to drape it across the windows of the entire carriage, acting on this Foster also unfurled his Union Jack although a lot smaller and draped across the windows opposite. This angered a lot of the other Welsh lads in our company. Most Welsh people hate the Union Jack and what it represents; the Union Jack is made up of the crosses of St. George, St. Andrew and the cross of Ireland but Wales is not represented. This is where a lot of the hatred stems from plus a lot of us Welsh see the Union Jack as pro England and not a British symbol.

A few of the Welsh supporters travelling with us charged towards us, "take that fucking rag down!" shouted one of the blokes at the front, they tried to rip the flags down but we weren't having that; we all stood in unison and confronted them, they stopped dead in their tracks and quickly realised they would have to come through us if they wanted to remove the offending flags; they were out of their league and quickly backed down and shuffled off to another carriage. The rest of the journey was uneventful; we pulled into Cologne station our numbers totalled one hundred with a hardcore of sixty lads. We dumped our bags in the station's lockers and made our way for a beer.

Inside the ground were a band of 500 hardy Welsh souls with a hardcore of 120 lads made up of the Soul Crew, The Wrexham Frontline, small groups of other North Walians including the Bangor lads. The German police had penned us in together, with little in the way of segregation. Once the main firm of Germans located us, they headed straight for us we could see them walking around the stadium towards us.

"Deutschland Hooligans! Deutschland Hooligans!" they screamed as they neared us, we readied ourselves, and prepared ourselves for the oncoming onslaught. We stood in front of them they outnumbered us 3 to 1; all I could see was a sea of bodies, a mass of flight jackets and leathers mobbed up in front of me. My stomach was in knots as we stared at them waiting for them to attack.

They steamed into us boots and punches flying wildly, there were so many of them attacking us a lot of them were hitting other Krauts in the confusion; all we could do was stand firm and try and repel this German army.

We had a good firm assembled, with main players from both the Soul Crew and the Frontline present. After the first attack I looked around and we were all still standing, staring defiantly into the faces of the Krauts before us; we called them on, they didn't need a second invitation and again they came steaming in, we battled toe to toe on the cramped terracing again forcing the Germans back and again there was a lull.

I looked at the German police, they seemed to be enjoying the entertainment and had no intention of intervening; I looked at the Welsh Police who had travelled over to monitor the situation and there was Jeff Richards stood baton in hand beating the Germans back; good old Jeff.

There was no let up from the Germans but every time they attacked, we would beat them back but still they came. We fought toe to toe all through the first half and I didn't see one minute of football, and it didn't look like the second half was going to be any different.

The attacks were taking their toll, we were knackered but we had no choice, while this wall of Krauts stood in front of us the harder we had to try to break through it, keeping on our feet was a must. Another prolonged German attack, we struggled to keep them at bay their greater numbers were starting to make a difference, and with the Germans starting to attack our flanks and forcing their way around the back of us, we started to take a hiding but we all pulled together and with another enormous effort we forced them back again. Again I looked around the lads, there were bloodied faces on both sides and as I stared at the Kraut directly in front of me, a couple of lads from The Frontline charged headlong into the Germans, they were taking the fight to the Krauts, unfortunately we didn't back them up quick enough and they were battered to the ground, as the boots rained down on them, Jeff the copper was straight in knocking the Germans back with his baton, although we were initially slow to react we were soon in the thick of the action, and dragged the Wrexham lads back to relative safety.

This was a defining moment and we all steamed into the Krauts; the look on their faces was priceless and they were soon on the back foot, I felt 20 foot tall knowing we had backed off three times as many blokes as us. The fighting continued for the entire ninety minutes and on the whole we came off second best; on the pitch we faired no better and went down 2-1. On the final whistle we left the stadium and went looking for the Krauts but the German police were having none of it, all the roads around the stadium were sealed off and the 120 of us were escorted to the train station.

The police put us on the train, but we managed to get off at the main station and to our surprise there were no police about so we made our way to the city centre and it wasn't very long before we bumped into 100 Germans. With the numbers in our favour the tables were turned, this was payback time, we spread out across the street, the Krauts were more hesitant than they were in the stadium, the same 120 of us steamed into them, at first they stood and it kicked off, one on one, toe to toe all over the street, both mobs got in amongst each other punches flew from both sides, we managed to smash through their front line and the Germans were on their toes, and although they regrouped and had a go at us many times throughout the night, each battle ended with us legging them into the darkness.

******

Unlike most foreign teams, the Germans did bring a small mob to Cardiff in 1991; we were drawn together again for the 1992 European Championships along with Belgium and Luxembourg; and before the game the Krauts were drinking in the Owain Glyndwr, which at the time was quite a notorious Cardiff boozer. We on the other hand were holed up in the Borough on St. Mary Street.

The Krauts were being a bit laery and word soon got around and a welcoming committee was sent to quieten them down.

It was about half an hour to kick off as we neared the boozer and we met the Krauts head on in a side street; there were equal numbers of us about 20 each but the Germans were huge compared to us. We faced each other, there was a short stand off, then one of our lot launched into this big bloke with a Flat Top hairstyle, that was our cue and we all set about each other, I was put on my arse by a muscle bound Kraut; the fight raged around me as I tried to clamber to my feet, while simultaneously dodging the incoming boots, these Germans were good and pushed us back towards St. Mary Street, as we passed the Old Arcade another well known boozer, another dozen lads joined us and with the additional numbers we managed to leg the Krauts up the street before the Old Bill turned up.

We made our way to the Stadium and took our places in the sold out arena and witnessed a piece of Welsh football history as we turned the Germans over 1-0 thanks to an Ian Rush strike.

Belgium 1991

Next up in this campaign was Belgium away and we were looking forward to doing battle with lads from Anderlecht and Liege; and once again loads of local lads of the IVF were travelling including Keith, Reesy, Foster, Bitten and Turkey plus a dozen others. They were travelling out as part of a large Soul Crew contingent that included a tight firm of lads from the Docks plus Pricey and Eifion from the Rhymney valley, these were two close friends of mine and real characters. Oz and I were travelling a day later, the plan being digs would be secured for us and we would all meet up on our arrival.

Oz and I met up with the rest of the Soul Crew at Cardiff Central Station, there were 80 of us in total and we were the B Team in comparison to the lads that travelled out earlier, although amid our ranks were colourful characters like Billy the Bus plus Bunjy and Deisel from Ynysybwl as well as a few main players dotted around including Karl who like us through work commitments had to leave late.

We made our way to Folkestone and caught the Hydrofoil to Ostend the crossing was a nightmare, gale force winds accompanied stormy seas and enormous waves came crashing down on top of the small craft; not being a swimmer I was concerned every time the craft became submerged. It was so rough the trolley dollies refused to come round selling their wares and I didn't dare venture from the safety of my seat to go in search of booze. Thankfully the crossing was very swift and I was overjoyed to get my feet on dry land.

We arrived at Ostend and boarded the train for Brussels, the journey was pretty uneventful, until we reached Luxembourg City. We pulled into the station the entire platform was full of local riot police all tooled up, an army of Robocops preventing us getting off, all this because we had rampaged through Luxembourg earlier in the year and they were determined to prevent any repeat performances, we all looked on in disbelief at the sheer numbers, it was if every copper in the city had turned out to welcome us.

As we neared Brussels itself we got talking to Karl, he was meeting the Soul Crew in the Midi District of the city, this is where our A Team were encamped, he told us Alan and his tight firm were arriving the day before the game. Alan and Karl always seemed to be in the thick of things at Welsh away games and this trip was to be no different. Oz and I on the other hand were meeting our mates of the IVF in the Centraal District of the city; Karl's stop was before ours and as he disappeared up the escalators we both knew we would be seeing each before the trip was over.

We arrived at Brussels Centraal station and deposited our bags in the storage lockers and went in search of the lads; and without the use of mobile phones the search was on, the first boozer we entered was a dimly lit, small quiet bar, we bought a couple of glasses of the local brew and went to sit down. It was then we spotted a dozen or so likely lads sat at the back of the boozer; all were dressed in the latest footy fashions and looked the part. Oz and I decided to join them and it wasn't until we neared them that we recognised them, they were Jacks, some of their firm's main faces, our faces said it all but we couldn't just turn round and fuck off, so we joined them for a drink. They knew we were Cardiff immediately, one of their lot recognised me from past battles; my heart sank I thought they were going to fill us in but to our surprise and to their credit we had an amicable chat with them. This was all they brought, a dozen lads and they were very wary of being located by the Soul Crew, we shared a couple of beers with them and left, but not before promising to keep their whereabouts secret. It was going to be a long couple days for them trying to keep a low profile but I wished them luck, they were certainly going to need it. I didn't go in for all this anti-Jack shit at Welsh games, I was all for an united front all Welsh together but sadly I was in the minority on that score.

We finally found our lads, holed up in another dingy boozer, they had secured rooms in a local hotel and we could bunk on the floor with them, sorted I thought and with that weight off our minds the serious boozing began, a pub crawl later and we met up with the rest of the lads of the Soul Crew in the Midi District.

We heard that the Docks lads had bumped into the Wrexham Frontline outside their hotel, the two mobs set about each other neither giving an inch, the ferocity of the skirmish was extreme with casualties on both sides, the local plod arrived, separated the warring factions and although there were winners and losers on both sides this particular altercation ended in stalemate. The police were operating a zero tolerance policy and all those involved were swiftly deported and that was the end of the good relations between the Soul Crew and the Frontline.

A few pints later and I was bladdered, I am a complicated person with a simple problem, alcohol, it has always been my weakness, some people get happy drunk others fall asleep while others get emotional I on the other hand get violent.

It was now time to trawl the local Kebab shops, the Midi District is awash with Moroccan and Turkish immigrants. We staggered into one of the many Kebab shops and I managed to get into a row with a Turkish geezer and proceeded to go over the counter at him and like all Turks he reached for the hardware and came at me with a blade, I tried to land a couple of punches on him while he waved his blade wildly, and with the help of my mates I was bundled out of the shop and out of the area, and Kebab was definitely off the menu. We headed back to our digs; the lads tried to calm me down on the way but I was having none of it and when we arrived at the hotel I kicked off again, this time with the hotel staff. Once again I was well out of order and a fucking nuisance.

The local Old Bill were duly called and I was escorted from the premises and arrested I thought that was going to be the end of my trip and that I would be deported but to my surprise I was released without charge first thing in the morning.

The day of the game everyone mobbed up in the main square; there must have been 500 Welsh fans gathered including a firm of around 200 Soul Crew. The booze was flowing freely, the atmosphere was good-natured and everybody seemed to be enjoying themselves. The boozers around the square were happy with our behaviour and happy to take our cash. A couple of hours later the riot vans arrived; the head honcho was in his mid thirties and dressed in a three quarter leather jacket, he looked nothing like the Old Bill at Ninian Park. He addressed the crowd and told us we were to be escorted to the Stadium. We had different ideas however, we had arranged to meet a firm of Belgians in a boozer near to the ground and twenty of us slipped off to catch a tram but our freedom was short lived. As the twenty of us sat there quietly peering out of the trams' windows we passed the escort and as the tram ground to a halt all eyes were on us, we were rumbled and thrown off to join the escort. The riot police took us on what seemed a tour of Brussels and two hours later the stadium finally came into view.

With two hours before the kick off we retreated to one of the many bars situated around the stadium; the police had us surrounded and there was no chance of mixing it with the Belgians, all our efforts were foiled, so it was back to the bar. Not having a match ticket, Hicksy and I remained in the boozer while the rest of the lads entered the ground. Wales came away with a credible 1-1 draw with Dean Saunders getting our goal. This was the best campaign we had enjoyed in years having taken points off all the top teams.

At the final whistle we met up with the rest of the lads and went looking for a bit of sport with the Belgians but the police had cordoned off all the side streets, and we were escorted back into the city centre.

A couple more beers beckoned and once again I found myself the worse for wear and isolated from the lads. In the main square as I sat alone on the steps of an old building trying to clear my head three Belgians approached me, they spoke to me in French, I didn't understand them but their tones were aggressive, I knew they wanted nonsense, I chose to ignore them while I figured out how I was going to get out of this situation, they kept on and one of them kicked my leg, I rose to my feet and decided to try and blag it by speaking Welsh, they weren't having any of it, one of them pushed my chest and grabbed my Burberry scarf so I lunged forward and shoved the head in with all my force. Suddenly I was grabbed and I took a couple of punches to my head, I swung wildly trying to connect with my attackers but a couple more blows to the head and I felt my nose break and I slumped to the floor, the warm blood ran down my face, I tried to protect myself as the boots flew in, one of them must have had a blade because I heard my leather jacket being sliced open, there were a flurry of slashes and I felt the cold blade run across my back, they stuck a couple more boots into me that connected with my head and they were off leaving me for dead; but not before relieving me of my cash, my sovereign rings and my cashmere Burberry scarf. I staggered to my feet covered in blood, disorientated and in great pain I slumped to the floor again and the next thing I was aware of was waking in hospital, luckily the blade had sliced through my jacket, jumper and shirt but had not penetrated my skin, I had got off lightly, that was the closest I've come to serious injury at a football match.

The Jocks

The Scots are our Celtic cousins and usually when we get together at social gatherings we get on well, we have much in common but the football is a whole different scenario.

The Jocks are renown for being big drinkers and having fiery tempers, and when this is mixed with the passion of their supporters all caught up in the emotion of the occasion its like a powder keg.

When our two countries meet it's a battle waiting to happen and we have crossed swords with each other a couple of times over the years.

The 1978 World Cup Qualifying round consisted of Czechoslovakia, Scotland and us; with the group winners going to Argentina. We played Scotland on 12th October 1977 at Anfield, and I settled down to watch the game on T.V. with my old man. The Welsh supporters were allocated the Kop End while the rest of the stadium was allocated to the Jocks but on the night the Welsh supporters on the Kop found themselves outnumbered three to one as the Jocks snapped up all the spare tickets; the Jocks turned Anfield into a home match with an overwhelmingly tartan atmosphere.

The police in their wisdom decided there was to be no segregation between the two sets of supporters. At first the banter was amicable and good natured but as Wales took charge on the pitch the atmosphere took a turn for the worse and while Wales dominated the early stages creating a host of chances which got the Taffies roaring and with the Welsh fans in good voice the drink fuelled Jocks started soaking the Welsh with urine and it wasn't long before the first punches were thrown and as the violence escalated the Welsh fans were subjected to a night of extreme violence.

Suddenly, empty Whisky bottles came cascading down onto their heads and there was a steady stream of blood soaked Welsh fans being led out of the Kop by the Stewards. The Kop soon became a cauldron of hate as the Welsh and the Jocks set about each other and the Tartan Army backed by their greater numbers battered their Welsh counterparts; it was a slaughter and things weren't going any better on the pitch with Joe Jordan's hand of God, the referee gave the Jocks a penalty which was coolly converted by Masson, this sent the Jocks into delirium while the seething Taffies attacked the Tartan clad hordes punching and kicking anyone within arms reach, the Jocks retaliated and their attack was merciless and relentless.

On a tragic night for Wales our campaign came to an abrupt end when Kenny Dalglish popped up to score and secure victory and qualification for Scotland, the Jocks were going to Argentina; while once again the Welsh supporters put away their passports; we were staying home.

Unlike nowadays where Firms go head to head this was indiscriminate with innocent fathers and their children bearing the brunt of the Scottish assault. Watching the match from the safety of my living room the full extent of the violence meted out was not apparent but in the next few days as the lads returned to the valleys with stories of the savagery and brutality of the beatings they took inside and outside Anfield a deep rooted hatred of the Jocks grew within the Welsh footballing fraternity.

The next major tournament we were grouped together was the 1986 World Cup Qualifiers, our group consisted of Spain, Iceland and Scotland, the prize was a trip to Mexico.

We were to play Scotland in 1985 to be played at Ninian Park; a 7:30 Kick Off on a sweltering summer evening. I had taken the day off and headed down to Cardiff in the early afternoon hoping to meet up with a few lads and get stuck into any Jocks that fancied it. To my horror all the city streets and boozers were full of Tartan clad, kilt wearing Jocks, the Tartan Army had invaded, so I headed for Cardiff Castle and there in the middle of the masses of Jocks; who were mainly stripped to the waist, was my good mate Mark H.

He was in conversation with three lads who like us were decked out in Burberry checked shirts and the fashion of the day; these were Aberdeen lads and they seemed to hate the Tartan Army as much as us.

We spent the rest of the afternoon regaling each other with past victories both on and off the field while supping a few pints. As Kick Off time approached we went our separate ways; Mark and I took our places on the Bob Bank; which in those days was a huge bank of terracing that held around fifteen thousand supporters. We made our way to the middle of the stand; this is where all the lads stood. Once again the police had deemed it fit for the Jocks to share the Bob Bank with no need for any segregation and the atmosphere was electric.

Firstly, the banter was good humoured but with no segregation it wasn't long before the two sets of lads squared up to each other. Our mob consisted of about 500 lads, about 200 youngsters of the Soul Crew, the usual faces that I'd travelled around the country with; plus about 300 older blokes; these were big lumps of men; miners and steelworkers from the valleys plus blokes from Barry and Cardiff Docks; we can always rely on the Shirters to get stuck in when it comes to a row. The Jocks had equal numbers, most of them stripped to the waist exposing their white beer bellies; these were older blokes too and most of them looked like they could row a bit.

Both mobs turned to face each other and steamed into each other; the whole terracing shook and the roar was deafening as punches and boots flew back and for; the brawl was reminiscent of a punk concert where everyone gathers in the middle and beats the fuck out of each other. We steamed into each other time and again and if anyone was knocked to the floor they were subjected to a brutal assault with everyone kicking and stamping on their heads and stricken bodies; I remained on the fringes while Mark was right in the middle of the action clouting the Jocks; sending them reeling backwards, I was biding my time waiting for my chance to pounce. Yet another Taffy onslaught and as the fists connected one sweaty fat Jock hit the deck; this was my opportunity, I rushed in and booted him in the head, I heard him groan as the leather connected, now I felt part of it the adrenalin was pumping; another charge towards the Jocks and I too was in the thick of it clouting anyone within my reach. The Jocks were taking a battering but they weren't giving an inch and just kept coming back for more.

The Old Bill tried to break up the melee but as they quelled one fight, scuffles broke out elsewhere on the vast terracing. The police were finding it increasingly difficult to get on top of the situation and the battle raged on. It was surreal how just a couple of yards in front of the battling hoardes thousands of normal spectators stood shoulder to shoulder glued to the action unfolding before them on the pitch and didn't give our antics a second glance.

On the pitch Wales were taken the game to Scotland and like off the field we were getting the upper hand and all the goal-scoring opportunities were falling to us. The Old Bill finally got the violence under control and I left Mark and went in search of other mates on the packed bank, and soon I found Andy from Dinas Powys; done up in his trademark Lacoste sweater; he hadn't got involved in the violence instead he chose to watch the football.

Around him were both Welsh and Scottish supporters mingling freely, there were no bad feelings and the atmosphere was much more relaxed. Wales were still having the better of the on field action and were creating more clear-cut chances but still the game remained 0-0. The packed Bob Bank bounced to the sounds of Welsh chanting and singing and the violence of earlier was all but forgotten. The Welsh team were doing us proud, yet another attack, the ball was played into the Scottish box and its in; 1-0 to the sheep-shaggers, the Bob Bank went wild, the Jocks were silenced, Andy and I were up in the air and as we celebrated a black Doc Martin boot came through the crowd and struck me on the thigh; I noticed the kicker; a Crombie clad skinhead who was stood a couple of rows in front of us, further down the terracing. Andy noticed the look on my face and tried to calm me down but I was having none of it; I made my way through the crowd and positioned myself to the side of the sneaky Jock skinhead and as he watched the game I gave him a right-hander to the side of his head; he flinched; he stared right at me; I stood there; the look in his eyes gave him away; his arse had gone, he didn't want to know, so I gave him another fucker for good measure and rejoined Andy.

It wouldn't be Wales if there wasn't any controversy and late on after relentless Scottish pressure the referee awarded the Jocks a penalty for handball where clearly the ball was played against our players' hand and after Welsh protests Scotland scored the resulting penalty to send the Tartan Army into ecstasy and the final score was 1-1; meaning Scotland qualifying for Mexico and once again our dreams went up in smoke.

Sadly, Jock Stein the Scottish coach suffered a massive heart attack and died in the stadium. At the final whistle, while the Jocks celebrated us Welsh made our way sullenly back to the train station, the mood was sombre as we trudged the long walk back to Cardiff Central. Inside the station concourse we met up with the Aberdeen lads from earlier; they had changed their tune they were now gloating over their victory; so I told them we too had gained a result, with the death of Jock Stein that was one less Jock to worry about; not surprisingly I was given a slap to my jaw which sent me reeling back a few steps, my first reaction was to get stuck into him but quickly realised that I was well out of order, so I just shuffled off to Platform 6 to catch my train home.

The only other meeting with the Jocks recently was a friendly in 2004 at the Millennium Stadium, which we won 4-0. The Jocks only brought around 40 lads, mainly Hibs and they were well shepherded by the Old Bill and apart from a few scuffles on St. Mary Street the day passed off without incident.

Dublin 1990

Wales were playing the Republic of Ireland in a friendly in Dublin; and with it being only a friendly there was little interest from the majority of the Soul Crew, so it was going to be just small groups of lads making the journey.

Bitten, Oz, Turkey, Sutton and I were travelling over together; Sutton was the weakest link, he wasn't a regular City supporter, he wasn't into the violence either but he was a regular in our local boozer The Castle Ivor plus he was a nice enough lad. Once in Ireland we had planned to meet up with Foster, Rees and the Bangor lads.

I had never been to Ireland before and I was really looking forward to the trip, especially because my father's family originated there plus the Welsh Egg Chasers were always telling us what a good welcome they get from the Irish, they journeyed over to Dublin every two years for the Rugby Six Nations competition but like I've said before football is a whole different ball game.

Bitten and I were really close at this time and were socialising together frequently away from the footy scene, plus he had started following United with me; he was one of the gamest lads I'd ever met and in all the scrapes we had been involved in I had never seen him back down from anyone; he was a real character the type once met never forgotten, he always left an everlasting impression on you, he was the type of bloke you loved to have standing with you in a row.

We had arranged to meet up early and make our way to Cardiff; have a couple of pints while the other lads spent the day at work but we very nearly didn't leave the valleys; as we were walking towards Pontypridd train station with our Head bags slung over our shoulders a police patrol car stopped us in our tracks wanting to know what we were up to, where we were going and more importantly what was in our bags, because we were well known to the local plod they went through our bags with a fine tooth comb but finding nothing out of the ordinary we were allowed on our way.

Bitten and I met up with Turkey and the others and we caught the train to Fishguard for our overnight sailing to Rosslare; on the way we had to change trains in Swansea. Once in Swansea we had just under an hour to wait for our connection; looking around the cold vast station our numbers totalled only twenty, made up of lads from Merthyr, Aberdare, a handful of lads from Newport plus King Tut and the lads from the Booze Crew, these were die hard Welsh supporters who would follow our national team to the end of the earth but these blokes couldn't fight their way out of a corner and as we stood on the concourse of Swansea station I felt rather vulnerable.

We decided to have a couple of beers in the boozer opposite and being just a score of us we kept a low profile, the last thing we wanted was to bump into a mob of Jacks and have a beating before even leaving Wales. To our surprise Swansea's streets were deserted and the Jacks never showed and our short stay in enemy territory was uneventful.

We set off to Fishguard and onto the ferry to Rosslare; the crossing passed without incident and we spent our time in the bar slowly drinking ourselves senseless. We docked in Rosslare and caught the connecting train to Dublin; the trip was turning into a booze trip with non stop drinking; with a shed load of booze and very little sleep we staggered out of Dublin station where we were met by a large ginger haired Irish bloke dressed in a three quarter length leather coat, he looked like someone who would have connections with the I.R.A. he asked if we had anywhere to stay, we told him we hadn't so he took the five of us for a pint and sorted us out digs in a local Youth Hostel. We dropped our bags off and headed for the boozers and the Dublin nightlife, hoping to meet Rees, Foster and the lads from Bangor.

We met up with Foster and the lads in one of the many bars on O'Connell street, their numbers were well down on our estimations and as we chatted we were told that the Bangor lads had been attacked by the Wrexham Frontline during the crossing from Holyhead. There had been a small group of Bangor lads, a handful from Colwyn Bay, Holyhead and Rhyl and forty Frontline aboard the Ferry. The Frontline sought out Joss and the others from Bangor and after a small disagreement the Frontline set about them, there was nowhere to run or hide and the Bangor lads took a good beating. There had never been any love lost between the two groups but of late Welsh lads had been far more united, this was a return to the bad old days and with our small numbers we all felt pretty vulnerable but on the other hand we wanted to avenge the attack on the Bangor lads and luckily that night our paths never crossed.

The following day was the day of the match and we had arranged to meet Rees and the lads at a boozer near Lansdowne Road. We all awoke feeling rough after yet another heavy night on the pop and we headed for the boozers around the stadium, although I personally didn't want to see another pint let alone drink one but you can't be seen to let the side down.

As we neared the stadium all around us were Irish supporters decked out in either the green of their national kit or the famous hoops of their Celtic shirts; as we made our way through the crowd of bodies we finally got our first sight of the Wrexham Frontline. They were forty strong and they stood out like sore thumbs in their flared jeans, hooded jackets and baseball caps as they marched down the street towards us; they had purpose in every step, the five of us looked at each other and we figured that they were looking for us and other Soul Crew lads, so we put our heads down, split up and mingled in with the crowd and went in search of our mates, luckily we had avoided them this time but I was sure our paths would cross sooner rather than later.

Two boozers later and we finally mobbed up with the Bangor lads, Rees and Foster our numbers now totalled fifteen, we were still vastly out numbered but I personally felt a lot more comfortable. I forced a pint down, a touch of Dutch Courage; our numbers might have been low but there were no mugs amongst us, every one of us could be counted on.

Around half an hour before Kick-Off and with the bar rapidly emptying, all the excited Irish supporters rushed out to take their seats in the stadium, as we looked out of the boozer's large front window, there in the street outside were the Frontline; this is it I thought, we all rose together and made our way outside; at first the Wrexham lads didn't notice us but then we were spotted, the street was still packed with Irish supporters slowly making their way to the stadium. The Frontline moved towards us their intentions were clear, we stood our ground and spread out, the Irish walked around us as we stood in the road, the Frontline also spread out, most of their top lads were present; lads we had stood with in Germany, Holland and Belgium.

The Irish supporters were mystified they didn't understand what was happening, for football hooliganism was virtually non-existent in the Republic. The Frontline were eager to get amongst us and they made their superior numbers count; but as we advanced on each other, it was one of the Bangor lads who threw the first punch and it was off, the Frontline steamed into us, we stood our ground as best we could; the Irish supporters scattered allowing us to get on with it. Punches and boots flew in from both sides and within seconds the Garda were on the scene, the Frontline pushed us back a little and a couple of our lot were put on the floor; I looked around at our lads; their faces told the story, it was time to run, we quickly backed off down the street; the Garda quickly came between us; the Frontline didn't give up though and tried to break through the Garda to have another crack at us; while we were just happy for the protection. The Frontline were very persistent and a few of their lads managed to make it through the Garda and the violence broke out again; once again it was the Bangor lads who were straight in. The Garda were unlike British Police and took no messing and soon had a number of Wrexham lads in the back of their vans, plus they had handcuffed one of the Wrexham's top lads to a lamp post while they tried to disperse the rest of the Frontline; while the Garda were dealing with the majority of the Frontline two of the Bangor lads had set about the handcuffed lad, punching and kicking him, he tried to kick out at them but it was to no avail and he took a bit of a beating until the Garda reappeared and dispersed us.

Inside the stadium there were about 400 Welsh and the Garda managed to separate the Frontline from the Soul Crew and there were no further outbreaks of violence and the game passed off peacefully with Wales losing 1-0 to a penalty. We left the ground and headed for the city centre bars and another night on the lash and although we had lost both on and off the pitch we were still in good spirits. The beer stuck in my throat; thankfully we managed to avoid the Frontline and the rest of the evening was spent in the company of our Irish counterparts who were good hosts and very laid back and were more interested in the Craic than causing trouble which suited us fine. The following day we were leaving Dublin's fair city, so we checked out of the hostel and headed for the train station. At the station we met up with Ferris and Gwylom; both of whom I had known since the early eighties and Ferris in particular; he was renown for his binge drinking while Gwylom was a regular traveller with the I.V.F. even though he wasn't interested in the violence side of things. Ferris was still bladdered from the night before but he still managed to bark out orders to an Irish station porter who was transporting his trays of lager on a pallet, also dotted around were Fussel and the lads of the Booze Crew plus old heads like Lug and his mates. We boarded the train and settled down for the journey home, the beer was still flowing, the five of us had drunk enough over the previous three days so we gave the booze a miss; Ferris on the other hand was knocking back his cans like they were going out of fashion. We arrived at Rosslare and went for a beer in one of the local boozers; while we waited for our connecting ferry we enjoyed a quiet pint but our thoughts were of getting home, we were exhausted, three days of virtually non stop drinking was starting to take its toll but needless to say Ferris and Gwylom were still going strong.

We boarded the ferry and headed for the bar, as the crossing progressed the more we got into the party mood; there were about 40 Welsh lads on board and the atmosphere was friendly and after talking to the other lads it seemed that it was only us who had trouble with the Frontline but after learning of our escapade there was an unanimous feeling of hatred and revenge and I knew that the next time our paths crossed the Frontline were in for a rough ride. The time spent on the ferry seemed to fly by and we soon found ourselves back in Fishguard; Ferris fell off the ferry and staggered to the train that was waiting at the station for us.

By now, the booze was in full flow and we were slowly working our way through Ferris's trays of Lagers, after a belly full of booze it wasn't long before the football chants started and to the majority of ordinary passengers aboard we must have been a pain in the arse. Further into our journey the Booze Crew joined us and they were soon challenging Ferris to a drinking competition; by now he was truly bladdered but he had a reputation as a big drinker his binge drinking exploits in the Rhondda were legendry; he worked hard and played hard. He took up the challenge with relish, although by this stage we were all bladdered we still had the sense to advise him against it, but Rhondda pride was at stake. The amount of grog he had already consumed was frightening and he was clearly on the verge of alcohol poisoning but he wouldn't be talked out of it. The challenge itself was to drink a 75cl bottle of Vodka on its head; he took a sip, then a gulp, he opened up his throat and swallowed half the bottle, he took a short rest then a couple of large gulps and the bottle was on the table in front of him empty; he took a large swig of his can of lager trying to get rid of the taste of Vodka from his mouth, he wiped his mouth, a large satisfied smile cracked out over his face, he slumped back in his seat and closed his eyes. We were all knackered, the booze was taking its toll; around twenty minutes later we noticed Ferris was covered in sweat, he was awake but rambling, he tried to join in our conversation but he was incoherent, he staggered out of his seat and aimed for the toilets but as he stood in the aisle he clutched his chest and collapsed. We surrounded him, his pulse was weak and his eyes had rolled back into his head, we knew he was in trouble. One of the lads went to get the train conductor who in turn phoned the police and ambulance service; the rest of us put him in the recovery position and waited for help to arrive. We all sobered up pretty quickly; the train came to a halt at Whitland train station in Carmarthenshire in the heart of west Wales; the first to arrive was a young copper who took a good look at Ferris and took his pulse by this time we thought the worst but he kept reassuring us that Ferris would be O.K. Time ticked by so slowly and there was no sign of the ambulance, we grew increasingly worried, as well as agitated and angry at the lack of assistance for our mate.

The ambulance and paramedics finally arrived over an hour later and our worst fears were realised; Ferris was dead, he had suffered a massive heart attack; I would like to take this opportunity to tell Ferris's family and loved ones that all of the lads that were present did everything they could to help him. Personally, I was full of many different emotions and the alcohol heightened them all; grief, helplessness and most of all anger, which was aimed at the paramedics because we couldn't understand what had taken them so long. The way the paramedics treated Ferris's body also angered us, they wrapped him up in a sheet and began transporting his body off the train, his lifeless body hit the seats on either side of the aisle and when Bitten complained one of the cheeky fuckers replied "he's dead, he can't feel it", Bitten swung for the bastard and luckily for him the copper was still on board or there could have been another death that night. The copper came between Bitten and the terrified paramedics and managed to escort them off the train and to the awaiting ambulance; once alone on the train our anger intensified and Bitten immediately threw a fire extinguisher through one of the windows, that was the trigger and we all got stuck into trashing the carriage, we worked our way through the entire carriage putting each window through as we went and the solitary copper could do nothing to stop us. The carnage continued for about twenty minutes, until we were all exhausted, we slumped in our seats amid the empty carriage surrounded by shards of glass; the silence was only broken by the sound of police sirens and a number of riot vans came screeching into the station car park. We knew what was coming next, we just sat tight while the riot police boarded, they came charging down the aisle and dragged the five of us off the train, we were bundled into the riot vans and taken to the local nick where we were interviewed.

During the interviews Sutton fingered Bitten and myself and although the rest of us remained tight lipped the Old Bill were happy to jointly charge the two of us with criminal damage. They held us overnight and we were bailed to appear at Whitland Magistrates Court a few months later. At the time of the court case Bitten was already in prison; he had got himself into an argument with one of his mates after an all day drinking session, Bitten carried out a ferocious and frenzied attack beating him to the ground and proceeded to beat him unconscious. He was sentenced to eighteenth months in Cardiff Prison but because of his frequent fucking about he had been transferred to HMP Swansea and additionally lost the opportunity of parole and early release. I had hired a car and Oz had agreed to drive me the 110 miles West. We were on in Whitland Magistrates at 9:30 a.m. so we left at the crack of dawn; I wasn't sure what to expect, I had been to court on numerous occasions but they were all violence related this was different I hadn't really spoken to my brief but I had decided to plead not guilty. We arrived in the town nice and early, finally located the Magistrates Court, which was located in the town hall. I quickly found my brief who informed me that Bitten wouldn't be attending due to a countrywide Prison Officers strike. Our case was adjourned and it was at this point my brief got the venue changed to Carmarthen Crown Court.

This was a testing time for me, my missus had just given birth to my son and this court case couldn't have come at a worse time.

With the court date looming I hired another car and Rob Foster had agreed to drive me to Carmarthen; these trips were costing me an arm and a leg and I couldn't wait to get it over with. We arrived at court, the local television and tabloids were present and more importantly so was Bitten. It was soon our turn in the dock; we were both jointly charged with causing a £1,000 worth of criminal damage. My brief had been working behind the scenes, he had struck a deal with the Prosecution; Bitten nodded to causing all the damage and I was acquitted; Bitten was sentenced to 12 months to run concurrently with his present sentence; Bitten had come through for me, and had made a selfless sacrifice.

Bitten went back to HMP Swansea while I went back to my family; looking back I suppose I neglected Bitten while he was stuck in prison and I don't think he's ever forgiven me not even now.

Years later Ferris's widow and family successfully sued the Ambulance service for negligence.

The English

During the Home Internationals Championships the biggest game of the tournament was our fixture with our sworn enemy and neighbours the English and being only four full time professional Welsh teams in the English pyramid every week brought us face to face with our English counterparts and the hatred on our part was always intense. We hate the English with a passion.

Football Hooliganism was once described as "The English Disease" which they exported all over Europe, leaving European cities trembling in their wake. So bad was the English reputation that our fixtures could only be safely policed if played midweek in a bid to stop the hooligans on both sides from travelling in great numbers.

My first Wales versus England encounter was at Wembley in 1981; another midweek fixture. There wasn't much interest from the majority of Welsh supporters; for many this would mean taking a day of work and most couldn't be arsed with the inconvenience.

Four coaches were booked; two organised by the Cardiff City Supporters Club plus two private coaches; one from the valleys and the other from Barry. The coach I travelled on was full of valley skinheads; this was before the Casual look took hold within the football fraternity. I travelled with my mate Slough both decked out in Stapress slacks, Donkey Jackets and Docs.

We arrived at Wembley Stadium; we pulled into the large coach park; this was my first visit to Wembley and the first glimpse of the Twin Towers filled me with awe. Thousands of English blokes were milling around, we made our way up the infamous steps and into the ground only to be told that there would be no segregation because of the low turn out. Once inside the ground we found ourselves isolated in small groups, we were in the lower terracing behind the goal; we kept our mouths shut as we were well outnumbered and surrounded by the English; luckily for us most of the lads were Luton Town so they didn't pose too much of a threat.

News started filtering through that a group of Welsh lads had been battered on the tube, this made us all feel a bit uneasy; the game kicked off and within five minutes so had we, the older lads steamed into the Luton; they were caught by surprise, the fighting spilled into the sparse empty terracing but after a frantic couple of minutes the Old Bill had the situation under control and we were escorted to the upper tier where another 300 of us were housed.

The game finished 0-0 and I knew that the fun was about to start; the Old Bill cleared the English from the stadium and the 350 of us huddled together waiting for the police to let us out. We knew that there would be hundreds of lads waiting to pick us off including lads from West Ham, Chelsea and Millwall. The Old Bill gave us the nod and we slowly shuffled towards the exits; the older lads headed the escort, they were skinheads who were the main hooligans of the time, Slough and I were tucked away safely in the middle of our group; there were about 70 of us youngsters who over the next few years would form the backbone of the Soul Crew.

We got outside and found ourselves surrounded by a mob of a thousand English thugs all baying for our blood; the police didn't want to know and it was every man for himself, a fight broke out in front of me as the English closed in on us; they attacked us from all sides, all the top London firms were present; we fought our way into the car park. The police managed to keep the majority of English away from us but one section of lads comprising mainly of Chelsea lads broke through the police; at the front was Hickmott and his mates; scuffles broke out around our coaches; Slough and I were just relieved to get aboard in one piece. In the darkness we could see blokes from our coach having it toe to toe with the English. Hickmott was forcing his way onto our coaches, a couple of lads at the front forced him off and closed the doors, we had managed to hold our own and fight our way out of a corner. The Old Bill soon secured the car park and to our relief we were able to make our way back to South Wales.

The following year it was the turn of Ninian Park to host the corresponding fixture another midweek meeting; the Soul Crew by this time was fully established and we waited to see if the English would venture into Wales in large numbers; this was a great opportunity to test ourselves against formidable opposition.

We mobbed up in The Philharmonic close to the Central station plus we had numerous spotters dotted around reporting the latest news. The English were arriving in small groups, which were well protected by the large police presence, with no sign of any action and kick off time approaching we headed for the Ninian Park pub; there were already a large contingent of the Soul Crew outside the boozer; a couple of English coaches passed by and were attacked with lads of all shapes and sizes trying to get aboard; the police had their work cut out as English fans were attacked as they parked their cars in the many side streets of Canton. Welsh lads were using the old chestnut of, "you got the time mate" to suss out the English.

Inside Ninian Park the atmosphere was highly charged, you could feel the hatred between the two nations. In 1982 the Falklands War was still raging and us Welsh chanted "Argentina, Argentina" because although there are a few Welsh regiments the majority of Welsh lads would never fight for an English Queen or even a German one as in Lizzies case and even less would fight under the Union Flag which us Welsh are not represented. These chants wound the English up and they charged towards the fences that separated us and the atmosphere intensified.

The game ended in a 1-0 defeat for us and at the final whistle we rushed outside into the large car park opposite there must have been more than a thousand waiting for the English to appear. We knew the Old Bill would try to disperse us, as they entered the car park they were met with a hail of bricks, at this time Cardiff were one of only a few firms that were happy to go toe to toe with the Old Bill.

After a couple of baton charges we were pushed out of the car park and up Ninian Park Road; sporadic outbreaks of violence continued all the way to the top of the road and the Old Bill were pulling loads of lads. The English were finally allowed out; those who had come by train were heavily escorted, they slowly made their way to the top of Ninian Park Road.

Meanwhile, the Old Bill forced us towards Canton and Riverside a direction we didn't want to be going in; we tried to break through the lines of Old Bill and get back onto Tudor Road to attack the English escort. Unknown to us a group of around 300 English had managed to slip their escort and we met them head on at the junction of Tudor Road. There was a short stand off and the English attacked, this was the best mob I had seen; England seemed to have lots of coloured lads with them and one of them in the front was a giant and he was whacking anyone who got near him. They ran through us like a hot knife through butter; they were a lot older and more organised than us, a lot of us were teenagers and we were soon on our toes leaving the bulk of the fighting to the older lads amongst us. The English soon had our older lads on the run and they chased us back over the Taff bridge and towards the train station. I had just got out of the hospital having had my appendix removed and I could barely run and I didn't want to get caught and the thought of being caught on the bridge and being thrown into the river Taff below frightened me to death; I could hear fights breaking out behind me but I couldn't turn around; I was glad to see the back of that bridge and to get into the bus terminus. I met up with a mob of around 100 lads and we attacked the English as they came over the bridge; we steamed into them but after a couple of brief scuffles we were on our toes again, we were scattered across the length of the bus terminus so I made my way to the train station a bit sharpish but I didn't feel safe until I was aboard my train heading out of Cardiff and back to the valleys.

That was one of the last times we played England because the Home International Championships were scrapped partly due to the arrogance of the English and the Scottish who thought Wales and Northern Ireland weren't good or worthy enough to play and partly because of the hooliganism that occurred in those fixtures, so the next time we met the English was when we were drawn together in the same group for the 2006 World Cup.

Northern Ireland, Austria, Azerbajhan and Poland made up the rest of the group but it was the matches against England that stirred the imagination of the lads and we waited in anticipation for the fixture list to be announced.

It was England away first to be played at Old Trafford because Wembley was still undergoing major renovation to restore it to its former glory; followed by the return meeting at the Millennium Stadium in September 2005, as soon as the dates were finalised we couldn't wait to mix it with the old enemy but the Football authorities had a surprise in store for us.

Only 7,000 tickets went on sale to us Welsh and the majority of tickets fell into the hands of the Welsh Travel Club Members and those on the Welsh Supporters Database; so for hooligans like myself it was going to be an uphill struggle.

The tickets sold out as soon as they went on sale and there were only going to be a small number of hardcore lads travelling to Old Trafford; most were going by coach; the lads of the PVM planned to arrive at Deansgate and have a pre match row with the English.

The day of the game however didn't go to plan, the Old Bill were on top of all the battle buses and directed them straight to Old Trafford. A couple of minor scuffles kicked off around the stadium before kick off, with the lads from the Ferndale Con Club right in the thick of the action but a number of Welsh fans who arrived at Manchester Piccadilly via the football special were given a rough time by the English lads lurking close to the station and on the whole the English took this piss picking off the Welsh fans with ease.

A lot of lads opted to make a weekend of it and a group of my mates had the same idea; they chose to stay away from the city centre but they found the local boozers were far from friendly. The Friday evening Charlie, Zak and Andy (The Spotter) ventured out to a local boozer which soon filled with Stone Island clad lads most of whom wanted to fill them in, so it was a night of keeping their heads down and trying to go unnoticed. This was not an isolated case Psycho from Neath and his mates booked into a city centre hotel but they too got a frosty welcome from the locals and found it safer to stay in their hotel.

After the match the police escorted our lads back to Piccadilly without major incident but the weekender lads had to keep their wits about them as they mingled through the hordes of English lads itching for a row but thankfully they all got back unscathed but the return match in Cardiff was going to be very interesting as the majority of lads talked of revenge.

******

The day of the game was a sweltering Saturday afternoon in September; I arrived in our capital just before midday. The train station was packed with both sets of supporters mingling freely the majority were normals wearing their teams' colours. I passed the police spotters and headed for the many boozers on St. Mary Street; the police had assembled a temporary football village in Coopers Field behind the castle for the English supporters; in a bid to prevent violence breaking out.

The whole of St. Mary Street was awash with red and white as us Taffies soaked up the pre-match atmosphere. I made my way to the Borough a known haunt of the Soul Crew; there amongst a group of top lads I found Jesse; he had his ear to the ground and had been on the mooch for most of the morning; he had spotted 40 Pompey lads holed up in the Life Bar, there were also mobs of West Ham and Bristol City dotted around the city but the majority of the English could be found drinking in the hospitality of the Football Village.

I left Jesse and made my way to the Gatekeeper on Westgate Street a stones throw away from the Millennium Stadium; there was a mob of around 600 of the Soul Crew's finest, everyone who was anyone was there, the majority of them in their thirties it was a proper rogues gallery. Some of the lads I hadn't seen since the late Eighties; this was an awesome firm, the last time I saw Cardiff pull a firm like that was away to Millwall at the New Den.

All the top lads were out; a pocket of English lads had been spotted drinking in one of the small boozers opposite the castle; so our mob was on the move, we advanced up the street the 600 of us moving as one; the Old Bill filled the top of the street in front of us with their riot gear at the ready. We advanced towards them; pint glasses and bottles were hurled towards them; the sound of smashing glass echoed throughout the street; the Old Bill charged at us and it kicked off lads against the police; I thought this was a good time to fuck off as lads were being nicked and bundled into awaiting police vans; Cardiff has CCTV Cameras on nearly every lamp post within the City centre and I didn't fancy an early trip to the cells. There was much more fun to be had so a group of about thirty of us slipped away from the carnage; leaving Sicey and his Valley Commandos to battle it out with the Old Bill.

The thirty of us headed towards St. Mary Street headed by Psycho, his brother plus other lads from Neath and Port Talbot; there were no novices amongst us; once on St. Mary Street we were met by a large police cordon. The English were well protected and the boozers on the castle side of the city were no-go areas for us Welsh but you can never give up; next we tried one of the many shopping arcades. The thirty of us silently made our way through the Victorian arcade trying not to draw attention to ourselves; it was like a game of cat and mouse, we managed to infiltrate the English-only zone undetected and there immediately ahead of us were the same number of English lads drinking al fresco soaking up the Welsh sunshine. These were lads no normals or shirters; we walked onto them one of our lads greeted them "Afternoon ladies", they let fly with bottles and pint glasses; we steamed straight into them sending them reeling backwards; once their ammunition ran out the English weren't so brave and after a couple more punches most of their lads were on their toes. The braver of their firm stood their ground and were met with another onslaught and they too joined their mates backing off down the street. The Old Bill were soon all over us and it was time to make a sharp exit and luckily all of us escaped the clutches of the Old Bill and made our way to the City Arms where I met up with Guff, Joss and the Bangor lads plus Pricey, Faggy and Mickey Villain top blokes each and every one. The English lads in the city kept their heads down and were barely seen; as the streets around the stadium started to clear and the stadium itself started to fill; there were still around sixty of us at the City Arms who were either banned from the footy or had decided to give the match a miss. We watched the match on T.V in the boozer and England soon went 1-0 up, the English supporters went wild with a number of them in the Welsh ends. Scuffles broke out all over the stadium and the English were unceremoniously turfed out of their seats and one English bloke in particular was beaten out of his seat and into the aisle, he was then beaten down the steps with a mob of Welshmen queuing to get their hands on him, he was continually punched down the concrete steps and at the bottom just before he got to the safety of the stewards a large Welsh girl stepped up and punched him full in the face sending him reeling down the last few steps; fucking priceless.

The half time whistle went and the majority of us lost interest in the match and went outside in the sunshine; a number of lads inside the stadium had the same idea and joined us outside the City Arms and our numbers grew to around 100. Days like these are not just about the football or the violence it's a social gathering and it's about the camaraderie, I can't properly describe it but once you are part of the firm your membership's for life, you're always welcome and it's a time to catch up with old mates.

It was not only us Welsh lads giving the game a miss; shortly into the second half we were joined by half a dozen lads who turned out to be the Lincoln Transit Elite; what a shit name for a firm; one of our lads had a word in their shells and advised them to fuck off for their own safety but they were having none of it; so quickly a stand off took place. We fronted each other face to face same numbers on each side; they were big lumps and I thought they were either brave because of the number of Old Bill milling around or they were fucking suicidal; after a minute of threats a large valley lad lunged forward and cracked one of their lads heads. We all surged forward but before it could fully kick off the Lincoln bottled it and were running up the street towards the safety of the police with half a dozen Soul Crew hot on their heels. Once the Lincoln disappeared the police gave us all a lecture and we returned to drinking and watching what was left of the second half.

The score line remained the same and at the final whistle we were joined by Dai Hooligan and his tight crew including Harris, Trajic and Dai Jones and we immediately headed for the English exit where we met up with another small group of top blokes from the valleys including Robbie, Rees, Tec and Elf. The English filed passed us in their thousands all proudly wearing their pristine

National shirts; we stood out like sore thumbs; the English knew who we were but were happy to walk on by. Fifteen minutes we stood there and all we saw were shirters; the English Travel Club has a lot to answer for.

Disappointed by the lack of English lads and with no sign of an English firm we headed back into town, we heard that a number of English lads were holed up in the Owain Glyndwr so we headed for their boozer; as we drew near it was already kicking off; other Soul Crew had beaten us to it the English were in disarray and were soon on their toes and we only caught the final moments of the altercation and soon the Old Bill were moving us on our way.

Minor scuffles continued throughout the evening with English lads coming unstuck and to be honest I was very disappointed with England's turnout; there was no comparison with the English firms of the heady Eighties but with the universal heavy policing it is getting harder to travel in large numbers. Overall the introduction of the English Travel Club, the English Football Village in Coopers Field and the professional police operation all kept violence down to a minimum.

CHAPTER EIGHT

WHEN IT COMES ON TOP

The worst part of football hooliganism is learning to accept and live with coming unstuck; it's a professional hazard; every firm in the land have come unstuck and been turned over at some time. When it does come on top it can be for a number of reasons:- simply being in the wrong place at the wrong time; being overwhelmed by larger numbers; having suicidal tendencies or simply being second best.

The worst scenario of things coming on top is when the Old Bill kick your front door in at dawn and parade you in front of your family and neighbours; and lately most major firms have known this feeling; plenty of firms have come unstuck and undergone high profile court cases resulting in top boys being imprisoned or receiving substantial banning orders.

More and more firms are finding it almost impossible to travel in large numbers; Battle Buses are now virtually things of the past, with the Old Bill contacting coach companies on the eve of matches, plus ever present Old Bill on the rail network; more firms are resorting to turning up on opponents manors with a skeleton crew of around fifteen to twenty lads, leaving them wide open to getting turned over.

Like a dozen or so Soul Crew diehards travelling to the likes of Wigan, Tranmere and Stockport on Friday nights; getting sussed by the home lads and trying to stand our ground on windswept empty station concourses against overwhelming numbers before having to run for our lives down pitch black railway tracks not knowing where we were running or what we were going to run into. With our hearts bursting through our designer gear and sweat oozing out of every pore; gripped by a fear of enemies everywhere and you daren't stop running or turn around. Here are a few instances of firms coming unstuck

The F.A Cup

Over the years we have had a few eventful FA Cup ties and one such match was on a rainy January in 1998 against Reading. Reading are a funny team; they are only a couple of hours up the M4 but they never bring any lads to Ninian Park; this was to be no different.

They turned up. Around 500 supporters including about 20 lads. After the match Pasti, Turkey, Steff and I headed for the city centre; it was absolutely pissing down so we dived in the Square Club on St. Mary Street where we were joined by a lad from Neath who told us that a mob of Reading were in the Wellington Bar on Caroline Street. There were only five of us so we had to rustle up a few more lads but with the appalling weather there was no one around; we finally found a few like minded souls and we were in business. Our numbers didn't even add up to ten. The plan was mapped out by the stranger from Neath; we would enter the boozer make our way to the bar and way up the situation.

We entered the boozer; the Neath lad took the lead, Turkey and Pasti were next then the lads we had rounded up and Steff and I were at the rear. We pushed our way to the bar; we passed a Reading lad and Turkey gave him a slap; he was rattled and the whole pub stood up. We were isolated; these lads weren't Reading though, these were boxing fans, watching their boy in the CIA Arena; they came straight at us. The Neath lad was straight into them, they came at us from every angle it was everyman for himself, I took a couple of punches to the face, it was getting heavy, we were getting smashed and had to fight our way out of there. I came face to face with a stocky bald bloke who took up a boxing stance, he came at me swinging lefts and rights and a couple of slaps later and I was sent flying through the large double doors. I turned to steam back in but Turkey came flying through the same doors, he had taken a couple of big punches and a boot up his arse for good measure, we both stood shoulder to shoulder in the rain ready to give it another go but we were soon joined by Pasti; he too was sent sprawling through the door; Pasti's a big bloke 6ft 5 and 18 stone, he was like Bambi on ice, he was sent reeling trying to keep his balance on the slippery wet floor. Turkey and I squared up to a group of boxers who had by now joined us outside, once again we received an hammering and as more boxers joined in it was time to split and we were chased down Chip Alley.

Turkey and I found sanctuary in a boozer called the Cottage on St. Mary Street where a little later we were joined by Pasti and Steff. We sat in silence still shocked from what had just happened but luckily none of us were seriously injured and after a while we could see the funny side of events and had a good laugh.

Boro 1994

With each FA Cup comes a certain excitement; especially for teams in the Doldrums like Cardiff, there's the chance to go on a successful cup run to bring in much needed cash and for us hooligans a chance to pit our wits against a top firm.

In 1994 we drew the Boro, this was perfect, a chance to win on the pitch plus a chance to go toe to toe with the Boro Frontline; anyone in the know respects the Boro, they are one of the top firms in England.

I got into the capital about midday and just my luck I bumped into the Boro firm as we left the station; they were an ugly looking firm with plenty of lumpers, these lads were the real deal. I followed them to St. Mary Street where they piled into The Albert, I nipped into the Downtown Bar opposite, there were usually plenty of crew in there; unfortunately there were just a handful of youngsters so I headed for the Owain Glyndwr.

There were 50 old heads and main faces dotted around the spacious bar; they were already aware of Boro's presence in the city and lads were scrambling around attempting to get more numbers. Around this time a lot of our firm had started drinking in Canton which is closer to the ground but personally I thought that for a game like Boro everyone would have mobbed up in the city centre but there again communication was never high on the Soul Crew's list of priorities and we must have the least organised firm in the country.

Around 2 O'clock we were joined by Reesy, Keith, Adie and other IVF lads, they had been drinking upstairs in the Albert when the Boro piled in; Boro had around 100 lads who like us were all old heads and our lads had managed to sneak out before it went mental. Our numbers totalled 70 this was it; time to make our move. We made our way down St. Mary Street; we had a good tight firm, most of the main faces were present and although we didn't have great numbers we were still quietly confident of getting the job done.

We advanced towards the Albert; I had butterflies in my stomach, we marched on in silence, the Docks lads were in front while I joined Rees, Keith, Adie and the other valley lads at the rear. We stood opposite the Albert; we could see the Boro inside, the Docks lads attacked the front doors, the Boro tried to force their way out onto the street. Try as they might the Boro couldn't get through the line of resistance and were pegged back inside the tiny corridor of the old pub. The valley lads and I were still stood in the middle of the road watching the battle play out before us; punches being thrown by both sides and suddenly the Boro burst out amid a hail of bottles, bar stools and punches; the two rival firms went toe to toe with one on ones breaking out all over the front of the Albert. More and more Boro charged out into the middle of the road bringing the

Saturday traffic to a standstill as the battle raged on; a large group of terrified shoppers watched the carnage unfold.

A group of Boro burst towards us headed by a large lad in a red jacket, Reesy and I steamed straight in, Rees's blows landed first catching him around the head, followed by a couple of mine; in front of me stood a lad in a black leather jacket; we attacked each other both landing punches, we backed off each other, I looked around me and although there were about 170 lads in the street only 30 of each mob were actually trading blows.

The Albert had now emptied and Boro's full firm were stood opposite us; behind me were the rest of our mob, who didn't seem to be doing much to help us. The Boro charged as one they steamed through the Docks lads at the front, they closed in, we were the last line of defence. There were about 20 of us stood in their way; I didn't know what to do, my heart said stand but my head said get the fuck out of there, so I decided to take my lead from the lads stood at my side. The Boro neared us and the 30 lads behind us had disappeared, our front line had been smashed, I saw a couple of our lads back off and we all turned and ran. I took refuge behind the pedestrian barriers when this giant of a bloke vaulted the barrier; he looked fucking evil; everyone around me were vanishing, we were chased down Wood Street; we tried to regroup and have another go at the Boro but this was more of a saving face exercise and once again the Boro ran through us.

The Old Bill escorted the Boro to the stadium, on the way they passed the Ninian Park pub where a couple of hundred Soul Crew were boozing; the Soul Crew attacked the back of the escort; we have never been worried about steaming through police lines but these minor scuffles were soon quelled by the ever efficient South Wales Constabulary and the rest of the day passed off without incident.

The Wurzels

Two of our great rivals are Bristol Rovers and Bristol City and over the years there have been some major battles between our firms.

Bristol Rovers

My first visit to Eastville must have been in the early eighties. Pughy, Big Ron, Slocombe and I travelled by train among a mob of around 250 Soul Crew all up for a day of Wurzel bashing. We alighted at Bristol Temple Meads station to be met by a large police presence; the four of us held back and managed to slip the escort and went looking for a boozer. We thought there would be hundreds of Cardiff dotted around, like us, left to our own devices but after an hour of traipsing around Bristol with no sign of familiar faces our brilliant plan was turning into a nightmare. We found out later that all later trains had been diverted to Stapleton Road. We were still wandering around slowly making the couple of mile walk to the stadium, when further up the street were a mob of 70 lads; none looked familiar to me but Slocombe recognised a couple of lads he had apparently met on holiday. I wasn't convinced but Slocombe was very persuasive so we crossed the road to them, a small group of them ran over to meet us, "Alright lads?" said the largest with a thick Brizzle accent; oh fuck I thought; the same thought must have raced through Slocombe's head as he answered in the worst Wurzel accent I had ever heard. We were sussed and the lad stuck the head into Slocombe's face; blood spurted out of his mouth, he reeled backwards, tears welled in his eyes. This is it I thought, Pughy and I assumed a fighting stance while Big Ron fucked off like a rocket; for a big bloke he could move; his donkey jacket disappearing into the distance. The Rovers' lad gave Pughy a dig, Pughy fronted him so he hit him again; he turned to me "Do you want some as well?" I declined his kind offer so he gave me a boot up my arse and told us to fuck off, which we did a bit sharpish.

We tried to keep our heads down as we neared the stadium but we almost got another feeding when we encountered another 30 Wurzels; luckily on this occassion we were able to give them the slip.

Inside Eastville, there must have been 6,000 Cardiff crammed into the three large enclosures behind the goal; just before the kick off the Home End erupted with a flurry of punches and boots and a large gap opened up; around 40 Soul Crew had infiltrated the Gas Heads and were taking the fight to the Wurzels. "Cardiff Aggro" came the chant from us, while the lads nearer the front of our End attempted to scale the perimeter fencing to get onto the pitch. The fight spread across the large terrace as running battles erupted and the rival mobs chased after each other, it was mayhem with flying kicks a plenty.

The Old Bill soon rounded up our lads and shepherded them out of the Home End and across the pitch; as they neared the Away End I recognised a number of the lads Mickey Villain, Prune, Lurch and others from Ferndale; before they could reach our end a group of Gas Heads piled onto the pitch from the side enclosure and a battle broke out in the penalty area. Ferndale's finest soon steamed into them and after a couple of slaps the Rovers were sent running back to the safety of their home enclosure.

At the final whistle around 250 Gas Heads steamed round our End and started smashing up the many coaches and vans in our car park; we charged through the line of Old Bill and kicked through the steel gates that kept both mobs apart and piled into the car park. The majority of the Rovers were on their toes immediately but those that did stand were beaten, kicked and trampled in the stampede as they became overwhelmed by our sheer numbers and there were many Rovers lads strewn all over the car park.

After chasing the fleeing Gas Heads for what seemed like ages we were finally rounded up and escorted back to Stapleton Road train station.

The game itself was a blur, only Jeff Hemmerman; our star striker breaking his leg in a collision with the Rovers' keeper stuck with me.

******

The next time I ventured to Eastville was in the early Nineties. Chilli and I left Porth early; this was a barren time for Cardiff City and support was dwindling but there were still about 200 Soul Crew on the Service Train to Bristol. While travelling; there was plenty of talk of going on the Rovers' stand and mixing it with the Gas Heads but once at the stadium only two dozen of us managed to blag our way in.

Chilli and I took our seats and we noticed there were no Rovers' lads in the stand; they were below us on the terrace but it wasn't long before some of our lot made themselves known and the Gas stormed up the steps to join us. We were outnumbered by 2 to 1 so we had to stop them getting in amongst us, we stood at the top of the steps using the height advantage. The first Wurzels up the steps were real big lumps, I clouted the first Gas Head while Chilli leant over and clouted another, they took a number of blows but they still pushed up the steps towards us; a couple of their lads were knocked to the ground and were trampled as the Wurzels kept coming. There were no Old Bill to be seen and the fight continued with both firms trading blows; my arms were getting heavy and after another tirade of punches the Gas finally forced their way onto the stand; we were all on the same level now and going toe to toe; more and more Wurzels steamed into us and we were finally beaten back; half of our lads retreated to the top of the stand while the remainder of us battled the oncoming Gas Heads. Chilli and I were still trading blows with the Wurzels while the rest of the lads fled up the stand; the Gas were swarming all over us so Chilli and I leapt onto the terrace below and battled our way through the Rovers and forced ourselves onto the pitch. Safe at last; I looked up into the stand, the battle raged on; the Gas had advanced up the stand and were taking the row to the Soul Crew; our lads were boxed in at the top of the stand they had retreated as far as they could; the two mobs set about each other with neither side giving an inch. The Old Bill finally arrived forcing the Wurzels back across the stand into an adjacent block; while the twenty odd Soul Crew were protected for the remainder of the match. The rest of the day passed without incident; the Soul Crew sometimes think their invincible but that day we ventured into enemy territory and came unstuck.

A few seasons later Rovers left Eastville to play at Twerton Park in Bath and although I visited there many times there was never the same buzz and I never witnessed any violence there.

Bristol City

You can't mention the Rovers without recollecting battles had with Bristol City. In February 2000, we played Bristol City at Ninian Park in a midweek evening fixture.

I took the day off work and headed to Cardiff; once in the city I headed straight for the Prince of Wales and met up with Pasti, Dion and Pricey. We had a mob of around 30 lads the majority of whom were like us valley lads; Pasti had the mobile number of one of the Wurzels, so we were in constant communication with each other and we were able to monitor their journey to the city. Around 3:30 the Wurzels arrived at Cardiff Central station and the Old Bill were to escort them to the Fly Half & Firkin a large boozer on Westgate Street. However, we had other ideas and we intercepted their escort on Wood Street; the Wurzels had equal numbers and we set about each other. The Old Bill were woefully unprepared; they battled to restore order as scuffles broke out all across the road, both mobs giving as good as each other. Finally, the Old Bill baton charged us and forced us back towards the Prince of Wales; while the Wurzels were led back towards the train station.

Our mob split into two groups; the first pursued the Wurzel's escort, while the rest of us made our way through a thin lane to an alleyway that runs parallel to Wood Street; our timing was perfect; we charged up the alley coming out in the middle of the Wurzel's escort; Pricey took the lead, while I was at his side, he steamed into the middle of them; the looks on their faces said it all they were shitting themselves, he gave one a good slap sending him reeling backwards then he caught another putting him on his arse, within a couple of seconds it was all over. The Wurzels scattered; those that stood got done; the majority of the Bristol lads were chased back into the station. The Old Bill soon had us under control and marched us back to the Prince of Wales where we basked in the after glow of a job well done.

As the evening progressed our mob grew to over 100 and when it was time we marched on the Fly Half & Firkin where by now over 300 Wurzels were housed. The boozer was surrounded by Old Bill; there were dogs and the usual surveillance cameras in operation; we advanced up the street; the doors of the boozer flew open and the Wurzels came steaming out into the road; we charged the pub only to be met by a hail of glasses and bottles plus the odd baton from the Old Bill as they beat us back down the street. For the next 30 minutes the Soul Crew and the South Wales Constabulary went toe to toe and after a few arrests and a few cuts and bruises we were forced to retreat.

The match itself was easily forgotten and on the final whistle the Soul Crew made their way to the Grangetown area of the City and lay in wait for the Bristol escort. Violence soon erupted and the Wurzels were attacked with bricks, bottles, lumps of wood and anything else our lads could get their hands on. Once again the Old Bill came under attack as the Soul Crew meted out a vicious assault on the boys in blue and the mayhem and sporadic violence continued for well over an hour. This was a favoured tactic by the Soul Crew and many a firm have come unstuck on a dark winters night as they made their long trek back to the safety of Cardiff Central station. I've been to Ashton Gate on numerous occasions with the Soul Crew and have never managed to have a proper row; the Old Bill always seemed to be on top and the same at Ninian Park apart from the odd altercation the Old Bill always have these fixtures sewn up.

The Boys from the Den

When it comes to Millwall, Cardiff will always pull a firm. In the seventies Millwall dished out beatings to all and sundry and terrorised many a good firm at the Den with Cardiff being one of them. Millwall were known to be a tight knit firm from a particularly nasty part of South East London; unfortunately over the last decade the Old Bill have had things pretty much their own way and on most occasions have come out on top but still I personally make sure I am about for every encounter with the lads from the Den.

The first time I ventured to the Den was in the early Eighties; on police advice, the match was to be played on a Sunday afternoon. Andrew Watkins and I travelled with Adar Glas the Valleys Supporters Club.

We arrived at the Coach Park and joined the other coaches about 300 of us made our way to the Den; on our coach were Fat Dai, Bruno, Little Trevor, Mario and Gina these were the thugs of the day. While queuing to enter the Den a mob of 50 Millwall steamed down the bank towards us; Cardiff backed off at first; I was just sixteen and I thought I was going to die but seeing that we had the larger numbers the older lads got in amongst them and with the help of the Old Bill The Bushwhackers were sent running backwards.

On the pitch Cardiff carved Millwall wide open and we won 4 - 0; this pissed the Cockneys off and many of our coaches lost windows on the way home.

The next time we played Millwall was in the FA Cup in 1986 at the Den, I was part of 250 Soul Crew on the 8 O'clock service train from Cardiff. We arrived in Paddington nice and early and headed across London on the underground system; there was a large brawl around Kings Cross where a couple of Old Bill were injured and in the chaos that followed the Old Bill nicked a couple of Cardiff's top lads who were totally innocent. (The guilty party was one of my best mates and things got pretty hairy for us valley lads as we continued to follow our team.)

We were escorted to Whitechapel where we were held for over an hour until the football specials arrived and were then escorted en masse; over 2,500 of us marching towards the stadium; we passed a few of their lads but they were little concern to us.

Inside the stadium the match ended in a draw and at the final whistle fighting broke out with the Old Bill as we tried to get out into the street to mix it with the Cockneys; the Old Bill were having none of it and by the time we were allowed out the nearby streets were deserted and apart from a minor scuffle with a few stragglers at Whitechapel the journey home was uneventful. Millwall brought very few lads to the replay the following Tuesday and the evening passed off without incident.

The Autoglass Trophy 1996

It was a cold November evening in Cardiff; I had just finished work and headed for the Downtown Bar; there outside stood a dozen lads these were Millwall and I followed them to The Albert which is opposite; soon there was 50 of us: lads from the Docks, Ely, Neath and Port Talbot as well as a few valley lads all crammed into the small bar area, you could cut the tension with a knife; personally I hate these situations I would much prefer to fight and fuck off than get into conversation with the enemy.

The atmosphere was tense and awkward and it wasn't long before the first punches were thrown; the Neath lads steamed in and we followed and half of the Millwall got filled in, while the rest bolted into the street and legged it up St. Mary Street.

Later that evening the same Millwall lads attacked the Ninian Park and battled in the doorway with a small number of Soul Crew who prevented them getting in and in the fight that ensued the large glass doors got put through it kicked off toe to toe both groups refusing to budge before the Old Bill arrived and escorted the Millwall to the stadium.

The New Den 1997

Midweek a couple of weeks before Christmas and we're off to the New Den for the 2nd Round of the Autoglass Trophy. The Battle Buses were booked:- two from Cardiff and one from the Valleys; the majority of lads were from Cardiff, lads from the Docks, Ely and other rough Districts of the city; and 50 of us from the valleys thrown in for good measure. Our numbers totalled 150 with all the usual suspects you would expect for a night out in South London. We arrived in London around 5 O'clock a good two hours before kick off, with no Old Bill in sight; we couldn't believe our luck; we got a phone call telling us to go to the Elephant and Castle. We plotted up in a local boozer; there was no sign of The Bushwhackers, just carloads of lads on mobile phones darting around outside.

We were told Millwall only had 50 out and weren't in any hurry to come to us; we had done everything we could to get a row sorted; we couldn't wait any longer it was already 7 O'clock so we headed for London Bridge.

We alighted at South Bermondsey a short walk from the stadium; it was a dark, cold evening as we turned on to the road; the Old Bill marched us towards the ground. We could make out a group of Millwall further in front of us, both mobs moved towards each other; there were no Old Bill with their lot so they came towards us unchallenged; we charged towards them breaking through the police and out of the escort, a couple of scuffles and minor skirmishes broke out and the police fought desperately to keep the two mobs apart.

We neared the New Den and some of the Cockneys got into the escort a couple more minor scuffles broke out but neither mob got seriously hurt; police reinforcements arrived and the Millwall were forced back; that was game over and once again the Old Bill won the day. Inside the ground our numbers totalled just 200 the straight heads had given this one a miss.

Ninian Park 1999

August 1999, the first home game of the new season and the boys from the Den were in town, unbelievably the police were happy for the fixture to remain a 3 O'clock kick off. I left Pontypridd on the 10 O'clock train; I couldn't believe it, the four carriages were packed with the Valley's finest, everyone was out for this one.

The London train arrived just before ours and we caught the end of the Millwall escort they had about 50 lads the majority were old heads these were their top lads. The Old Bill corralled them in Sam's Bar, on the corner of the bottom of St. Mary Street on Mill Lane which is in the "Café Quarter", of the city.

We headed for St. Mary Street, the boozers hadn't opened yet but the Soul Crew were out in force; large gangs of lads roamed the streets, as our numbers grew the Old Bill cordoned off the bottom of St. Mary Street in an attempt to keep us and the Londoners apart.

Around 12:30 another train bringing another 150 Millwall arrived and were escorted to Sam's Bar; although the boozers were now open the majority of us were happy to stay on the streets.

The Bushwhackers were happy drinking and soaking up the August sunshine outside the boozer and were in no hurry to get into a confrontation with us and all the Old Bill's efforts were aimed at us and whatever we attempted we could not penetrate the police line. Finally we gave up and headed out of the city centre for the Poet's Corner in the Riverside area of Cardiff.

The boozer was rammed, with lads spilling out on the street; we had a good 400 lads assembled, all itching to get it on with the Cockneys and after an hour we made our move; taking the backstreets we headed into town; with our huge numbers I thought it would be only a matter of time before we would be sussed by the Old Bill; amazingly we marched unchallenged, a top firm heading for a row; we passed the rear of Central station and up Penarth Road; under the railway bridge and there opposite was Sam's Bar and outside stood 200 Millwall lads, we charged across the road at them; the Old Bill suddenly sprang into action; mounted police plus the riot cops charged towards us beating us back with their riot shields, only for us to fight back, there were too many of us and we broke through the police lines; we advanced towards their boozer only to be met with pint glasses, bottles and plastic tables and chairs but Millwall never once attempted to attack us. The Old Bill regained control before any punches were thrown.

The Old Bill forced us back down under the railway bridge using batons and shields to beat us towards the ground. We knew that the police would have to escort the Millwall via Penarth Road and through Grangetown and we chose the same route. The Millwall were about ten minutes behind us so we did everything possible to slow our escort down and fights broke out between us and the Old Bill as they tried to make us step up the pace.

We were walked passed a large park with a playing field and we all piled through the gates; this fucked up the Old Bill and Millwall's escort finally came into view only railings stood between us, as they were marched passed we charged towards them and fought our way through the Old Bill, we were stopped in our tracks when the police helicopter that had been overseeing the operation landed in the field in front of us; the power from the roter blades sent us scurrying backwards and away from the Millwall. The Old Bill finally restored order and held us in the field until the escort had safely passed; by the time we were allowed out on to the road the Londoners were away in the distance nearing the entrance to Ninian Park and the police ensured our two firms never met.

Once inside the ground the 200 Bushwhackers took their place on the Grange End terraces part of the travelling 1000 away support and throughout the ninety minutes missiles were thrown back and for. At the final whistle the Old Bill kept the Millwall support locked in while a mob 1500 hardened Cardiff hooligans congregated outside the Grange End exit; this was not uncommon at Ninian Park but on this occasion the Old Bill couldn't move us. Missiles flew back and forth over the fence and we could hear the Millwall kicking off with the Old Bill. It was total mayhem with lads surging back and for; the Cockneys were trying desperately to open the gates to get out amongst us, while we fought the Old Bill to get into the Londoners.

After about fifteen minutes of utter chaos the Grange End gates suddenly and slowly started to open; I couldn't believe my eyes the Millwall had broken through the riot police and were now in control, the gates opened further and a small mob of Millwall steamed out but they were set upon immediately, punches and boots flew into them, it went toe to toe until our superior numbers forced them back in.

Meanwhile, back inside the stadium some of the Bushwhackers had managed to scale the perimeter fencing and headed for under the Grandstand; the doors flew open and 50 old heads came storming out onto Ninian Park Road, right into the middle of us; the majority were stripped to the waist and a couple of them were armed with mops and brushes; they must have ransacked the cleaner's cupboard. They couldn't have known what they were about to bump into; once we had sussed what was happening and who was who we steamed straight into them from all sides and soon there were two South London lumps sparked out on the road and after a swift onslaught the Millwall turned and legged it back under the stand followed by around 400 Soul Crew all baying for blood. Underneath the stand the Cockneys were trapped, penned in and I found myself right at the front; we swarmed all over them, punches, boots we hit them with everything; they fought back as best they could but they were overwhelmed and by the time we backed off there were a group of South Londoners lying in a heap some of whom needed hospital treatment. The Old Bill were soon battling through the crowd and cleared the scene; that was the worst beating I have ever seen a firm take it was brutal nothing more than slaughter.

The New Den December 1999

The return fixture was in December and all police leave in London was cancelled to ensure there was no repeat of the violent disorder that broke out at Ninian Park.

The straight heads gave this match a miss and the 670 of us who travelled to South Bermondsey where made up of hardcore old heads, most of us had been waiting all season for this fixture. We knew the Bushwhackers would want revenge for the severe beating they suffered at the hands of the Soul Crew.

The Soul Crew was mobilised; everyone travelled by service train to London; only 20 travelled on the first train, the second train was filled with 350 lads the majority from Cardiff and its surrounding suburbs and the last service train carried 300 valley lads. Oz, Turkey, Pasti and I were on the last train; all the top valley lads were there:- Mickey Villain and the Ferndale lads, Little Dean, Boundsy and the Rhondda lads as well as lads from Blackwood, Neath, Port Talbot plus Pricey and the lads from the Rhymney valley.

Looking through the packed carriages there were lads I hadn't seen at the football for years; this was a final swansong for many of the older lads. Almost all of the lads were in their thirties this was a proper firm of mature old heads, all seasoned campaigners.

We finally arrived at Paddington; the police lined the platform some taking photographs, we marched up the slipway and onto the street; there in front of us were the lads from the earlier trains; our firm was pure evil, all intent on violence; Millwall would need to have their A Team out if they were going to mix it with us. The Met police escorted us to Paddington Tube station and onto Victoria where we needed to change platforms; this was to give the Met a major headache; considering our large numbers and the calibre of the lads present we had been very well behaved but this was to change when the Met started playing silly buggers with us; they tried to fuck us about slowing down the escort and pushing and shoving our lads at the rear until we were all squashed against each other and that was when the trouble started. The Met were pushing and shoving us with their shields and batons, and those of us at the front of the escort got a rough deal, it was reminiscent of the picket lines during the miner's strike; a roar went up "Kill, Kill, Kill the Bill!", it all turned nasty; it kicked off with both Old Bill and lads being wrestled to the floor. The Soul Crew in this mood takes some stopping and a number of police forces have come unstuck when they've tried to take us on; and the Met were going to find out the hard way; we smashed our way through the Old Bill at the front sending them sprawling to the floor; and the firm was off, out into the street we went, it was sheer mayhem, some lads took this opportunity to trash the nearby shops while others went on the rob. I couldn't help feeling that if the Met had played fair this could have been avoided. After about twenty minutes and with the help of reinforcements the Old Bill gained control and escorted us onto a tube bound for London Bridge and after another change of trains we arrived at South Bermondsey.

The Old Bill held us at the station and we could see the Millwall lads scurrying around in the streets below. The Met were finally happy to allow us to move on and we were marched the short walk towards the stadium. We passed the Cliftonville boozer; the Londoners inside peered out pressing their ugly mugs against the filthy windows. The Met kept our escort slowly moving towards the stadium, up ahead of us in the distance were the Millwall mob but the Old Bill had them under control and we were taken under the bridge to the ground.

At the final whistle we were held in the ground while the Met dispersed the marauding Bushwhackers. We were finally allowed out into the dark streets; and as we made our way back to South Bermondsey station we could hear the Millwall and the Met kicking off in the surrounding streets. The Old Bill took us back across the underground system to Paddington; when we arrived, I couldn't believe my eyes as hundreds of police flanked us and their numbers stretched the full length of the platform. It was the largest police operation for a league match in British Football history and not a punch was thrown all day; that's part and parcel of our game you win some you lose some and that day the Met came out on top.

Since we gained promotion to the Championship we have played Millwall many times but because of Millwall's reputation the Old Bill always advises the clubs to play midweek in an attempt to prevent the Millwall from travelling in large numbers and recently each time we've played at the New Den our club has made travelling a coach and ticket affair so recent fixtures between our two clubs have passed off without incident.

The Weekender

For about a two decades starting in the mid Eighties, I formed a strong, lasting friendship with a group of lads known as the IVF and we travelled the length and breadth of the country following our beloved City in shitty Transit Vans. We tried to visit Blackpool for a Weekender at least a couple of times a season. Usually we stopped off after away games in the North West.

One such occasion was our visit to Tranmere Rovers; it must have been in the early Nineties, it was the first away game of the season. We always put a firm together for the first game of the season; an opportunity to renew acquaintances after the summer recess. It was rare to play Tranmere on a Saturday, usually our fixtures fell on a Friday night so a lot of the lads had never been to Prenton Park and a chance to do a new ground always brought a number of lads out of the woodwork. Personally, this was an ideal opportunity for revenge because I had been turned over a few seasons earlier when a handful of us turned up by train; after the game we were attacked at the station and I was given a good feeding.

There were a couple of Battle Buses booked; while the IVF were travelling by transit van the plan was to all meet up in Blackpool for some post match hi-jinx.

There were fifteen of us all sound blokes; we had travelled together on many occasions over the years and been involved in many scrapes; I'd trust most of these lads with my life:- there were Keith, Reesy, Foster, Pricey, Adie, Froggy, Bexy Trueman, Hicksy, Summers, Kenny Ham, Gwyllob, myself and a few others. Our driver for the day was a lad called Hibberts who was originally from Nottingham but had moved to Church Village; he was always first to steam in and usually first on his arse, he was game as fuck and fancied himself as bit of a hard man but the truth was he wasn't much of a fighter.

The van was a complete shed but we were used to travelling in shit; we were all crammed in the back, no seats, just mattresses, blankets and our jackets for comfort.

We made steady progress and the alcohol and Class A's helped to take the edge off the long journey. We arrived at Prenton Park home of Tranmere Rovers; we passed a large boozer at a junction on the main road; this was their main watering hole, they had a mob both inside and out. Our van with Capel's Van Hire South Wales emblazoned on the side and back doors gave the game away and as we got stuck in traffic the Scousers made their move towards us. About 30 of them made their way through the stationary traffic but they hadn't bargained on us being tooled up. Hicksy and Summers put on their balaclavas and armed themselves with lead beaters; they flung open the back doors and started beating the floor of the van; the Scousers stopped in their tracks and jogged back to the safety of their boozer.

We parked up in the car park but we knew we had to pass their boozer to get into the stadium. We all kept together; keeping it tight as we passed on the opposite side of the boozer; the Scousers had large numbers about 150; we eyed each other up but they didn't make a move they seemed happy to let us pass.

Inside the ground we had 400 lads stood on the steep bank most of whom were going onto Blackpool after the game. We lost 5-1 and the drizzle started to fall on the open away terrace and once the fifth goal flew in we had seen enough and the fifteen of us made our way to the exits and to our surprise the Old Bill were happy to let us leave. Outside we were met by another twenty lads with the same idea; we soon made our way towards the home terrace; the gates were already open so we ambled up the steps and onto the large covered home end. We had a mooch about but the Scousers' firm were nowhere to be seen so we returned outside and waited.

At the final whistle the home supporters streamed out; the majority were straight heads; we had no problem with them. Within five minutes Tranmere's firm were on their way out, they were in the middle of their scarfers, they were unaware of us stood just outside the gates. They neared our position and we steamed into them; the front of their firm took the brunt of our assault; they didn't know what was happening; we knocked them backwards and in the confusion their normal supporters scattered, leaving us a clear path into the Scousers; most of their lads turned and ran; those that stood fanned out in front of us and we soon ran through them smashing them everywhere and finally chased them back onto their end.

The Old Bill were slow to react and by the time they appeared it was all over and as we walked passed them we couldn't help smiling.

We arrived in Blackpool around 7 O'Clock, parked the van and headed for the boozers; the excellent thing about Blackpool is it's a Hooligan magnet with different firms stopping off all the time. It's the constant unknowing of who or what will cross your path.

There were 150 of us mobbed up in a boozer just off the tower; there were the usual rumours flying around that Brum and Pompey were also mobbed up in town and after a couple of pints we decided to leave the main mob and embark on a mini pub crawl on our own. Personally I don't like rowing with huge numbers, you never know how good the bloke standing beside you is and whether he'll fuck off if it comes on top; give me these fifteen lads every time once they're in they're there for the duration or until the Old Bill arrive.

The fifteen of us made our way down the busy front passed the many Hotels and B & B's and the hustle and bustle of weekend revellers; after a few more pints the booze started to take its toll our little mob were all strung out; Froggy, Adie, Bexy and Gwylob were on the opposite side of the road; Keith, Reesy, Foster and the majority of the lads were a couple of hundred yards ahead of us while Pricey and I were at the rear. We carried on down the strip when out of a side street came a dozen or so lads; they were in the middle of us, Pricey said "we'll have it with this lot" and he steamed into the back of them; he caught one of their lads with a flurry of punches to the back and side of his head; I steamed in straight behind Pricey firing a couple of shots into the head of another unsuspecting lad; their lot turned to face us; and we were having it toe to toe with them; a flurry of punches landed on us; Pricey took a blow to the side of his head, we both were forced backwards they were all over us and finally Pricey jogged away into the middle of the road and I was left battered and I was dumped headfirst inside a large wheelie bin.

All this action was played out in front of our mates opposite who thought my demise was hysterical; while the bulk of our mob at the front walked on unaware of what was happening just 50 yards further up the street. Our opposing firm strutted off victoriously, and we were joined by our mates; Pricey was hurt quite badly he had suffered a perforated ear drum and a broken bone in his hand, while I luckily was only a bit bruised, I had got off lightly. We caught up with Foster and the rest of our lot and set out for revenge.

Their firm hadn't got far and we all steamed them from behind; Reesy smashed his way through the first couple and both mobs piled into each other. These lads were Leeds and they had a few big lumps among them; one lad in particular stood out he was a big ugly cunt with a face only a mother could love; he was covered in scars no doubt picked up in rows like this. It was toe to toe; we started to back them off up the street; Pricey and I were in the thick of it once again and we took our revenge on one of their lot who got isolated and after a few clouts he was on the floor; we pushed them further down the street and a few of their lads started to disappear but their diehards at the front stood their ground; ugly was still swinging punches; we rounded on them and Reesy smacked a couple more blows into them and they finally turned and fled into the neon lights.

Ahead of us was a Police van so we made tracks a bit sharpish and dived into a nearby boozer, we sunk a couple more beers and headed to the Tower Ballroom where we met up with the rest of our firm. Dotted around inside were a number of small mobs but our sheer numbers ensured they gave us a wide berth and the rest of the night went quietly and once again we had to endure a sleepless night in the back of our transit van; the smell of boozy farts and stale sweat permeating the air and although these were great times I couldn't wait to get home and jump in the bath.

Brighton & Hove Albion

Brighton Hove Albion might not have the biggest or most notorious firm and Brighton the town may well be known more for being the gay capital of England where one in three men are homosexual than for football hooliganism. But if you fancy a weekender and turn up mob handed you will undoubtedly come across plenty of stiff opposition; no pun intended.

Brighton Hove Albion are a small team with passionate supporters and are one of the few teams that always bring a large following to Ninian Park and at home they also pull together a decent size firm whenever we're in town.

I first travelled to the Goldstone Ground in the mid Eighties; around 160 of us left Cardiff Central early on a cold Autumnal morning; the Soul Crew at this time was still in its infancy and we were an unruly mob of adolescents with plenty of bottle but no organisation; we were still finding our feet as a firm in the shady world of football hooliganism. We had been involved in a few skirmishes in the previous season and at that time we were happy to run amok around English towns bumping into rival firms more by chance than through planning and Brighton was to be no different; we marched aimlessly around Brighton town centre looking for mischief, looting local off-licences and jewellers and generally enjoying the away-day until the local Plod stumbled upon us and we were escorted to the stadium.

Brighton were attracting large crowds around this time and the match atmosphere was electric; there were 1500 of us in the Away End including a firm of 300 lads; we were all bouncing and things were to get even hotter at the final whistle; the Old Bill were happy for both sets of supporters to exit the stadium at the same time and once we were out on the street our lot split into two groups, the train mob and the others.

The Old Bill began to escort the 300 of us towards the station and we had only moved about 100 yards when Brighton's firm appeared on the opposite side of the road and the two mobs steamed into the middle of the road. The Old Bill tried to keep us apart but battles broke out in the darkness; it was a free for all with lads of both sides as well as the police darting everywhere. It was hard to tell who was who until you were on top of them, the battle raged on as the police tried to restore order; around 50 of us fronted the Brighton and we steamed straight into them, their lads at the front were smashed backwards and the rest of their mob were on their toes into a nearby park; we gave chase and caught a few of the slower ones; including a short fat lad in a dark hooded jacket; who was knocked to the ground and was severely dealt with. The Old Bill finally caught hold of us, rounded us up and escorted us back to the station and on the train journey home everyone was retelling the parts they played in the row and we all felt invincible and when I stepped off the train back in Porth I walked down the main street with an extra bounce in my step and a strut instead of a walk.

****

We didn't play Brighton again for a number of years; a lot had changed they were no longer playing at the Goldstone Ground, that had been sold for redevelopment; their new home was the Withdean Stadium and their attendances had plummeted. The next time Brighton visited Ninian Park was in the late Nineties; it was one of the first games of the season and once again they brought a large following, the majority were straight heads all decked out in their teams colours and before the game they were in the city centre mingling with the City faithful basking in the August sunshine and the mood was good natured but all that was to change after the match. The police allowed both sets of supporters out the same time and the vast majority of Brighton entered the car park opposite and boarded their buses while a small number of straight heads made their way to the station. A few of these started getting lippy taunting the City supporters about the score; we had lost again; some of our younger more unruly element attacked these normals and some of them were given quite a beating before the local Plod rescued them and escorted them to the station and from then on Brighton have wanted revenge.

Brighton Away

The next time we played Brighton was December 2001; Pasti his brother-in-law Jimmy and I left Pontypridd early morning; the game was at the Withdean Stadium and was all ticket; the 450 tickets were snapped up by the Supporters Club so lads like us had to travel ticket less. We left Cardiff Central station; the train was empty, it seemed none of the firm were travelling so the three of us got a couple of cans from the buffet and settled down for the rest of the journey. We arrived at London Victoria where we had to catch our connection; having plenty of time on our hands we went looking for a boozer; Chelsea were playing Man United and Victoria was swarming with Chelsea who had filled all the nearby boozers so feeling a tad vulnerable we returned to our platform.

We boarded the train and met Gareth from Neath who was travelling alone; also aboard were a handful of loons from the Rhondda who were throwing as much fighting powder up their snouts as they could; these were the type who would start screaming Cardiff as soon as they'd get off and have the local Plod swarming all over them, so we kept our distance from them.

We arrived at Brighton around 1:30 and let the loons walk off the station first; immediately they started screaming and shouting drawing attention to themselves and suddenly the Old Bill were all over us like a rash; we were all searched and held at the station; opposite us was an Irish boozer where around 200 Brighton were plotting up; they had just rampaged through Trafalgar Street and had gone toe to toe with the Old Bill who had needed back up from dog handlers to quell the fighting. Brighton had pulled a top firm and were expecting a load of us on the train not the pitiful sight of just four lads; the Old Bill prevented the majority of their lads entering the station concourse but a couple of them managed to mingle with us but the plod split us up before we came to blows.

The Old Bill put us on a train to Preston Park; we arrived at our destination and there waiting for us were another forty lads and a large police presence and we were escorted the short walk to the stadium where the Old Bill were happy to let us in without tickets.

The Withdean stadium is a real shit hole; with an athletics track around the pitch, a large open banking, one main stand and two stands with temporary seating one of which was the Away End; which was uncovered and as the rain grew steadily heavier we stood huddled together getting soaked; we had a firm of around 60 who were growing more and more impatient as the game wore on and on the stroke of half time Bobby Zamora scored to put Brighton into the lead.

At half time Lakey and around a dozen lads were ready to exit the stadium, Pasti, Jimmy and I also wanted to be part of it but we missed them by a matter of minutes and the Old Bill locked the gates and we were confined to watch the rest of another dismal City display. During the second half a mob of 40 Brighton also left the ground and finally located our dozen lads in the Station Hotel; a listed building nestled in a side street of terraced houses. Brighton attacked the boozer smashing every single window and steamed the doors and attacked our lads inside; snooker cues, pool balls, ashtrays and even road signs were used as well as the pub furniture as both mobs fought it out. Our lads managed to force the Brighton outside and the fighting spilled out into the street both mobs going toe to toe with each other; both firms were picking up and using anything and everything they could lay their hands on and two of our lads received hospital treatment after large plant pots were smashed over their heads. The Old Bill were on the scene pretty sharpish and several Brighton lads were nicked.

After the match Pasti, Jimmy and I filed out of the stadium into the December darkness and headed for Worthing to meet up with Lakey and the others; they were holed up in a boozer they had drunk in earlier in the day, there were 50 of us and when the three of us heard what happened at the Station Hotel we were gutted and we wanted revenge, the Old Bill surrounded the boozer decked out in riot gear with shields and batons drawn. Around 7pm a firm of 50 Brighton also boarded a train bound for Worthing, arriving at Worthing station they attacked the local plod and escaped from their clutches by running along live railway lines, we could hear them coming through the streets, their roar getting louder and louder as they drew nearer and we could finally make out their silhouettes in the street lights. They were eventually intercepted as they reached the junction opposite our boozer; both mobs tried to get at each other through the police lines but the Old Bill charged into their firm cracking heads with their batons; Brighton were well up for a row and fought hand to hand with the Old Bill. Finally they managed to disperse the Brighton mob and more arrests were made before their firm were escorted back to Worthing station. The rest of the night passed off without incident and we headed back to Wales.

The Boys From The Port

As well as the Jacks and the Wrexham Frontline, Newport County also had a tight firm, during
the Eighties and early Nineties we had plenty of run ins with their lads. Newport is only 12 miles
from Cardiff and has plenty of rough districts to recruit lads from and even when Newport
County plunged into non league football their lads didn't give up the violence and they plied their
trade with teams in the top flight.

The County were always languishing in the lower divisions but in '82 they gained promotion to
the old Division 3 which meant there would be the first league meeting between our two clubs for
many years, both fixtures passed off peacefully mainly because County didn't travel to Ninian
Park and by the time the return fixture arose it was a top of the table promotion battle and we
swamped Newport with our sheer numbers and we came up against very little resistance.

By the mid Eighties we had been relegated to the lower leagues again we were a yo-yo club
around this time and we would face the County once more; this time County had an emerging
firm of about 200 lads pulled from the many sprawling sink estates also around this time
Newport's lads were starting to turn up in Cardiff on match days for a pop at us. The numbers of
the Soul Crew were dwindling with many lads giving the City a miss and concentrating on First
Division teams instead; myself included I could be found on the K Stand at Old Trafford
watching United more than at Ninian Park.

The County would turn up on our manor with 30 lads and end up going toe to toe with equal
numbers of the Soul Crew and they always gave a good account of themselves, they were never
given a good hiding and most rows ended all square.

The Welsh Cup Final 1987

The County had progressed to the Welsh Cup Final against Merthyr Tydfil a non league team
from the valleys; the match was to be played at Ninian Park on a Sunday Afternoon. A mob of us
from the valleys headed for the capital including:- Ashley, Cen, Johnny, Monster, Turkey, Bitten,
Oz and I; we knew that County would have their A Team out and this was an ideal opportunity
for them to take the piss in Cardiff.

We mobbed up in the Philharmonic on St. Mary Street which along with the Brownhills Hotel
was a favourite haunt of ours; we had around 150 lads mobbed up, we sipped our pints patiently
waiting for the County to arrive. Suddenly the scouts returned from the station and we were all
flying out the doors with half drunk bottles and glasses in our hands. Newport had arrived and

were making their way along Wood Street; we steamed around the corner and there they were at least 250 of County's finest stood just yards in front of us. We steamed towards them, the County stopped in their tracks; I was right at the front of our mob and my momentum took me bowling into their front lines; I swung out a punch; it connected with his face; he was older than me but looked just as scared as I was, I knew he was hurt as soon as I hit him and he crumpled to the floor. At the front of their firm were a couple of coloured lads; we were straight in amongst them, boots and punches flew from both sides.

Suddenly from behind us came the shattering of glass as the other Cardiff lads threw their pint glasses towards the County but they were hitting us as well and as we ducked for cover the County charged at us and the lads behind us legged it back into St. Mary Street; with everyone around us disappearing we had no option but to join them. We fled with the County close on our heels I could feel them getting nearer and I wished I hadn't had that earlier pint which was now in my throat. The County were closing in on me but luckily I reached the Cambrian Arms and sought refuge behind the bar. Newport chased the main mob of our lot up St. Mary Street and the stragglers who got caught were involved in ferocious scuffles on both sides of the road; this was certainly a good result for County on our own turf.

Inside the stadium itself was pretty quiet and the match was insignificant; we couldn't wait for the final whistle and mix it with the County once more. At the final whistle we all filed out together; there were large groups of Merthyr and Newport supporters donning their clubs' colours plus a mass of lads in the fashion of the day; Armani knitwear and Fiorucci jeans were favoured at that time and as both mobs merged together making our way from the ground it was difficult to tell who was who.

We came under the bridge near the Ninian Park pub; I looked around and there were just five familiar faces amid a sea of strangers, I whispered to Bitten "these are County" and suddenly it kicked off behind us, the Soul Crew had steamed into the County the battled engulfed us the five of us were swinging punches as if our lives depended on it. The County backed off to the opposite side of the road; our numbers were about equal. They had 200 stood outside the Ninian pub while we filled the road and pavement opposite. We steamed into them; County had a huge coloured lad stood at the front and Mark H headed straight for him and laid one on him, his knees buckled and that was the last piece of the action he saw that day. We pushed the County back against the brick wall of the pub; it got to much for a couple of their lads who legged it into the car park at the rear of the boozer but they were soon hunted down and given a good beating. The County that stood came unstuck and if the Old Bill hadn't turned up it could have been a lot worse. The Old Bill waded into us trying to make arrests; about 20 of us legged it from the scene to the junction by the park where we bumped into a dozen County who had appeared from one of the side streets; we spotted each other simultaneously and walked towards each other only two Old Bill were present and tried desperately to keep us apart but skirmishes broke out all over the road; the County lads were well up for it and although we had the larger numbers they never took a backward step. The Old Bill broke up most of the scuffles letting fly with their batons, I was whacked around the back of my legs; the fighting stopped and both sets of lads walked into town, with County on one side of the road and us on the other.

That was the last violence I encountered that day but we managed to restore some pride knowing that the bulk of County's mob were turned over outside the Ninian.

Orient Away

In the early Nineties City were once again languishing in the lower divisions and a lot of the main faces had dropped out of the scene and were more interested in the Dance scene and preferred to spend their weekends getting loved up on E's at Raves than cracking heads at the footy; the number of lads travelling with the City was in free fall; the majority that did still travel were young kids and Orient away was to be no different.

I left the Rhondda valley alone; none of my mates could be arsed; I arrived at Cardiff Central and met up with around 40 lads most of whom were kids in their late teens with just a few of us old heads dotted around; one being Gareth from Neath who was a bit older than me; he was one of our top lads and a good mate of mine; us older lads took our seats well away from the youngsters, got a couple of beers from the buffet and talked about present relationships and passed battles. We arrived at Newport station and a group of two dozen lads boarded and took their seats at the front of the train away from the bulk of us; Arsenal were playing United at Highbury and there was good support for both teams in Newport . We pulled into Paddington and arose from our seats the 40 of us left the main concourse and headed for the exit; there ahead of us were the two dozen blokes from Newport. A couple of our eager younger lads charged into the back of them swinging punches; the Newport turned and faced them; they were a lot older than our lot, the majority were in their mid thirties. They rounded on our lot and a couple of the youngsters were floored, the rest of us raced up the slight incline to get in on the act; both mobs went head to head; our lads might have lacked age and experience but they had plenty of guts and courage; us older lads joined the fray and took our place at the front, I squared up to a large bloke in a leather jacket; we both traded blows as the battle raged on around us. Within the ranks of the County firm was a mountain of a man; 6 foot 6 if not taller, he had fair shoulder length hair and a full beard; he had hands like shovels and he was whacking everyone in his sights; each of the lads he connected with folded under his power they either hit the deck or backed off a bit sharp. This giant was unstoppable he was working his way through our mob single-handedly until Gareth stepped in; he caught the big guy with a punch full in the face the big bloke didn't flinch he just swatted Gareth with a backhander and Gareth too beat a hasty retreat; by now there were only a handful of us still fighting and I was having my work cut out, every punch I threw I got two back; the County now had the upper hand and I watched helpless as all around me retreated back down the hill. I backed off too but got caught by a right-hander that put me on my arse and a couple of boots flew into me catching me around my head and upper body but luckily I managed to curl up and the onslaught was soon over and I was able to rejoin the lads back inside the station. There were a couple of us with cuts and bruises but most of the youngsters were more shaken than seriously hurt, for some of them this was their first encounter with a proper mob and they had received a harsh introduction to football violence. As we sat on the tube in relative silence us older lads stared at the shocked faces amongst us but today was going to be a defining moment for some of those lads; some we would never see again as they turned their back on life in the Soul Crew for others this experience would make them stronger and give them an added impetus to inflict beatings on other firms.

Pre-Season Friendly 2000

The next time I ventured to Newport was in 2000 for a pre-season friendly; Somerton Park was now a housing estate and County were playing at Spytty Park which was more of an Athletic Stadium than a football stadium.

I was working for the Civil Service at that time; Clive my work colleague and ardent Cardiff City supporter and I had decided to book a half days leave and head for Newport. Most male Civil Servants were up their arses and I found I had fuck all in common with the majority of them but Clive was different; like me he didn't take work all that serious and he didn't take any shit from anyone, he had a cracking sense of humour and he liked a drink; he wasn't an hooligan by any means but he loved the City and he would stand his ground if it came on top. I saw this at first hand when we both went to Merthyr Tydfil for a another pre-season friendly the previous season; at the final whistle while we were heading back to the railway station five local lads started taking liberties, Clive and I crossed the road towards them, they came at us as one; we squared up to them, their eagerness to get into us was their downfall; the first in got a smack on his beak off Clive and the next one came at me swinging. All his punches failed to connect and I hit him straight on his chin and he hit the deck and after a couple more blows from the both of us three of them were laying on the ground and the remaining two suddenly lost their appetite for the fight and scurried back across the street with their tails between their legs.

The day of the Newport fixture I arrived at work to find Clive dressed in a yellow City away shirt, orange Bermuda shorts and sandals; I knew he had no fashion sense but this was fucking ridiculous. After lunch we clocked out and caught the train to Newport and headed for a boozer on the high street; we enjoyed a couple of quiet pints when a handful of locals entered and after a quick mooch around the boozer they came over to our table; the biggest lad asked "over for the game?" I jumped in before Clive could open his mouth "no, we've just finished work, we're just having a pint before heading home" with Clive wearing a City shirt they knew we were lying but they left anyway. I told Clive to drink up before they came back.

We thought it would be safer if we made our way to the stadium, as we neared Spytty Park we bumped into the back of County's mob the majority were decked out in Stone Island; luckily they hadn't noticed us; I nudged Clive and explained what was happening, we tried to keep our heads down but this was easier said than done with Clive's City shirt sticking out like a sore thumb. As we entered the stadium car park the turn-style entrance was to our right, I pulled Clive's arm and shepherded him towards the entrance. A roar went up and the front of County's mob charged towards a couple of cars in the car park; A.A. a known face on the terraces at Ninian Park had turned up with 2 cars full of City lads. The County steamed straight into them; A.A. was their main target and soon the Newport lads were swarming all over him; the City lads were vastly out-numbered, there were only eight of them and one of them was A.A's missus and they were taking a good kicking. Clive and I looked on helpless and by the time the Old Bill arrived A.A. was almost out on his feet.

Clive and I entered the stadium; dotted around the entrance were small groups of County lads; they were onto us immediately; they left Clive alone but I took a couple of clouts and a boot up the arse for my trouble. In the main stand were Cardiff shirts and straight heads and I was getting too much attention from the County lads for my liking; I was an easy target and I didn't want to end up like our lads in the car park so Clive and I fucked off and stood besides the athletics track where we met a handful of Soul Crew from Blackwood and other surrounding Rhymney valley towns.

Just before kick off our numbers had grown to ten; A.A and his mates had decided to give the match a miss and headed back to Cardiff; the County lads numbered around 60 and they soon spotted us and were soon on their way towards us; there were only a couple of Old Bill inside the stadium and there was no segregation. The County took their place just a couple of feet away from us and after a short stand off Woody from Bargoed gave one of the County a dig sending him to the floor, we steamed into them and the customary gap appeared and after a couple of scuffles the Newport backed off and the Old Bill separated us.

About ten minutes into the match I received a call from my mate Pasti who was among 50 Soul Crew making their way to the stadium; they had arrived by service bus and had managed to give the Old Bill the slip; this news was music to our ears and we couldn't wait for them to arrive then the fireworks would start; but as they neared Spytty Park they put in the front windows of a local boozer and the Old Bill were soon all over them.

The Old Bill weren't the only ones alerted to our lots presence and soon there were 60 County heading in their direction. The Old Bill refused to allow our lads to attend the game and escorted them back towards the train station but our lads refused to cooperate and the escort proceeded at a snail's pace; suddenly the Newport came steaming out of a side street attacking the escort, the police battled to keep the rival firms apart, scuffles broke out all over the street. The escort ground to a halt as lads from both mobs kicked off with each other, both mobs steaming back and for through the line of the Old Bill. The police finally got on top of the situation and with the use of batons they dispersed the County and beat our lot back to the station.

Meanwhile, back inside the stadium our numbers had grown to 25 but with the additional Old Bill there were no further outbreaks of violence. At the final whistle we all filed out of the only exit available, we had to pass the remnants of County's firm and punches were thrown from both sides, sly digs in the darkness caught lads out, we crossed into the car park; scuffles continued between the parked cars; Clive and I kept our heads down and shuffled off towards the train station unnoticed.

CHAPTER NINE

CONCLUSION

The Lads

For nearly 25 years I have been a regular down the City and in that time I have forged numerous lifetime friendships and like any club its strength is its members and the Soul Crew is no different; it united lads from different walks of life and backgrounds, City lads and Valley lads; lads of all sizes and ages all bound together by a love for their football team and a love for good clothes and its been a pleasure to know each and everyone of them. The Old Bill and the NCIS might know them as Category C Hooligans or even criminals but to me they are simply mates and there is no doubt in my mind they have shaped my life and have made me what I am today, they have made a huge impression on me. I feel privileged to call those blokes my mates and looking back over the past quarter of a century I can honestly say I don't regret a single thing that I've done or been involved in and I'm proud to have stood at the side of these lads.

In the beginning Andrew Watkins introduced me to my first taste of football but as he dropped out of the scene in the early Eighties I teamed up with Slough, Pughy and Slocombe all down to earth valley lads all with a zest for life and a sense of adventure; this was in the days before the Casual scene took hold and we went to the City to simply watch the match.

1982, the Casual Scene went hand in hand with the football violence and The Soul Crew was born, the Rhondda Fashionistas were John Harris, Julian and Donald Trajic; they were a few years older than us and we all wanted to look like them; they were real head-turners. However, there were other dressers in the Rhondda; Lurch, Elvid, Prune, Mouldsy, Dai and Mickey Villain all hailed from Ferndale a rough mining town at the top of the Rhondda Fach while in the opposite Rhondda Fawr were Winkle, Dai Mogg, Elf and Robbie Bound strutting their stuff in the latest styles. The dressers I mixed with were Cen, Dukey, Ashley Lloyd and Johnny we all hailed from Porth and up until 1987 we were inseparable. Around this time we were drinking in the Champions Bar in Pontypridd with the lads from Hopkinstown; Bitten, Oz, Turkey, Dillys, Dai "Morphine" Morgan and Karl "Monster" Fletcher were the main players and with the help of us Porth lads we never lost a battle in Pontypridd. In later years we were joined by Pasti a former Pontypridd Mod his brother-in-law Jimmy and his nephew Steff plus Dion from the Aberdare valley.

We had also joined up with the I.V.F around this time and this friendship lives on today; throughout the Eighties and Nineties we hired numerous Battle Buses under the guise of shopping trips and Stag Nights and when we travelled with smaller numbers the Transit Van and Minibus was the chosen mode of transport. The I.V.F consisted of:- Reesy, Keith, Mark H and his younger brother Adie, Froggy, Nigel "Bexy" Trueman, who took his nickname from Gary Oldman's character in the 1988 play The Firm; Simon, Kenny Ham, Rob Foster and his younger brother Paul, Dai Ambler, Huw, Digger, Wurzel, Summers and Hicksy a band of lads from Taffs Well also played a part in our firm they were Lintern, Ginger, Granville and Titch.

Over the years as our notoriety grew with other valley lads, a group of game lads from the Rhymney valley pitched in with us and were regular members of our tight away firm these consisted of:- Pricey, Tec, Faggy, Stevie Woods and the lads from Bedwas this small band of lads were solid gold and Pricey still remains one of my closest friends.

The lads listed above and I all travelled under the I.V.F. banner; we were a smaller splinter firm of The Soul Crew and I wood fancy our chances against the same numbers of any firm in the country. Another splinter firm was the Pure Violence Firm of Port Talbot and with the lads from Neath they formed a formidable firm their main players were:- Huw, Guff, Anton, Psycho, Scouse, Gareth and Simon.

Another splinter firm were the Bangor Warfare Squad; we were very close to these North Walian lads especially at International matches and strong friendships were forged with this small band of die-hards, on their day they could pull a good 20 lads for the City cause; they usually turned out for games in the North West and Chester City and Wrexham always saw a full compliment of their Squad; their top players were:- Joss, Alwyn, Harvey, Kevin and Martyn.

However, lately I've been hanging around with the Party People of the Cave; Steve Eckhardt whom I've known since Bolton Away in 1987 and has been a sound mate throughout; Zak, Charlie, John the Postman and Andy "The Spotter" all top blokes and true City lads; the hospitality they afforded me was second to none and without lads like these plus other like minded lads throughout Britain the whole of the Eighties and Nineties would have passed off incident free.

The Last Word

Almost a quarter of a century I have been an active member of the Soul Crew and during that time I have noticed the police become more adept at tackling crimes associated with football hooliganism and over recent years the introduction of modern technology and more proactive policing as helped to dramatically reduce violence at the City. The Old Bill and the NCIS in particular have started winning the war on the streets and because of these victories the numbers within our firm have decreased. The days when you could land on a rival firm's manor mob handed and have a full-scale battle are long gone. The only offs that take place nowadays are between smaller numbers far away from the prying eyes of the Old Bill; these battles are still brutal and vicious but less frequent. Everything is organised these days and the mobile phone is king. gone is the spontaneity of the eighties and early nineties; the lads I knock around with are from the old skool and have never pre-arranged a row in their lives, that was part of the fun; not knowing what you were going to come up against.

As the 2005-2006 season draws to a close and another almost trouble-free Championship season ends the police are the only ones who have come out on top and even though the season brought encounters with the likes of :- Hull City, Leeds, Millwall, Wolves plus both the Sheffield clubs; all of these fixtures would have put us against some handy firms and would have guaranteed a row a few years earlier but with the introduction of I.D. Cards and Club Membership Schemes a lot of us were denied access to tickets and travel. So the club managed to stop the firms travelling in great numbers and to a certain extent ended the violence.

When we were operating during the early eighties the Transport Police were the closest to us hooligans and they kept dossiers on the main faces and knew most of us lads by name but the normal Old Bill didn't give a fuck about preventing punch ups at the footy; they relished the opportunity of overtime and the more sadistic bastards among them enjoyed the buzz as much as us.

Slowly over the years Police Intelligence started to improve and in 1988 the NCIS was formed and this led to better shared intelligence between police forces up and down the country. Each firm had their own Football Intelligence Officers assigned to them who would camp outside the main boozers and constantly take photographs of the lads; the Cardiff Spotters must have more photos of me than my family. They would also follow us in their bright yellow Hoolivan which was linked to CCTV monitors and Police Headquarters and even on non football days they'd turn up in the boozers and hassle us. With the Old Bill increasingly getting the upper hand this forced a lot of the main faces and old heads of the firm to take early retirement; sometimes you have to re-evaluate your priorities when you've got a wife and family you've got more to lose than gain; and with the judiciary handing out stiffer sentences a stretch over the wall was more than likely if you got fingered.

The net was closing in on us Category C Hooligans as the Old Bill collated more an more information on the main faces of the Firm. The Soul Crew was dealt a hammer blow when over 100 lads were pulled in Operation Javelin after our ill-fated trip to the Britannia Stadium at Stoke; dawn raids took place across South Wales based on video footage of events in and around the stadium; most of the lads were done for pulling at fences separating the rival firms, although a few were done for more serious offences such as assaulting the Old Bill. Some of the lads were given prison sentences while the majority received banning orders of up to ten years including some of my good mates.

At this present time Cardiff City the football club are punching well above their weight and holding their own in the Coca Cola Championship but Sam Hammam and the Club with their Draconian measures have alienated us lads; who in the dark days of the mid Eighties when the Club were playing in front of three thousand crowds were the bedrock of the club and we have been told in no uncertain terms our kind are no longer welcome; we don't fit into their corporate all-seater image. The season just gone was the City's most successful since the 60's, they were vying for a place in the play-offs with six games remaining but the team were watched at home by an average of only eleven thousand supporters.

I'd say at least 90% of hooligans love the Beautiful Game and their team with a passion unrivalled by anyone but I have noticed times when we had travelled to the likes of Millwall, Man City and Stoke got results on the pitch but were still disappointed because the Old Bill had things sewn up and the all important off had remained elusive; it's a strange feeling that I can't really explain but an anti-climax borne out of frustration. I still turn out for the bigger games but instead of attending the match I prefer to remain in our boozer with our banned lads and I am not alone; there are normally at least 50 of us left enjoying a pint and a chat about the good old days while the masses leave for the stadium. If I do attend a game its with my son who's 17 and luckily has no interest in the violent side of football but if he or any other youngster was contemplating running with the firm I would have to advise them against it simply because the Old Bill are in control these days and its only a matter of time before your caught and you find yourself facing either a lengthy stretch over the wall or a lengthy banning order; its just not worth it.

Although the NCIS are undoubtedly winning the war against football hooliganism I don't think they will ever fully eradicate the Soul Crew at Ninian Park the lads will always turn out for the big games either out of tradition or out of habit; I believe there will always be a firm of some description.

As for the future; personally I have come full circle, after watching a highly skilled World Cup I've got my love of the ninety minutes back and with our National team rejuvenated under John Toshack I look forward to the oncoming European Championships with relish and on the domestic front with Cardiff City making some promising new signings plus having the go-ahead from the local Council to start work on our new stadium in November this year; the future looks bright, the future looks Blue.

Printed in the United Kingdom by
Lightning Source UK Ltd., Milton Keynes
139942UK00001B/26/A